THE WEIRDEST SCI-FI COMIC EVER MADE

UNDERSTANDING JACK KIRBY'S
2001: A SPACE ODYSSEY

THE WEIRDEST SCI-FI COMIC EVER MADE

UNDERSTANDING JACK KIRBY'S
2001: A SPACE ODYSSEY

JULIAN DARIUS

SEQUART ORGANIZATION   EDWARDSVILLE, ILLINOIS

The Weirdest Sci-Fi Comic Ever Made: Understanding Jack Kirby's *2001: A Space Odyssey*
by Julian Darius

Copyright © 2013 by Julian Darius. Characters and works mentioned herein are trademarked by various owners.

First edition, May 2013, ISBN 978-1-4895-6618-8.

All rights reserved. Except for brief excerpts used for review or scholarly purposes, no part of this book may be reproduced in any manner whatsoever, including electronic, without express consent of the publisher.

The cover is a version of a NASA photograph of Jupiter and its moon Io. Book design by Julian Darius. Interior art is © Marvel Comics; please visit www.marvel.com.

Published by Sequart Organization. Edited by Mike Phillips. Thanks to Keith Howell, Markisan Naso, Richard Pachter, and Scott Puckett.

For more information about other titles in this series, visit Sequart.org/books.

Introduction

Jack Kirby's *2001: A Space Odyssey* is surely one of the strangest science-fiction franchise comics ever published.

For one thing, the comic appeared in 1976, *eight years* after the 1968 film debuted. In theory, the comic was timed to a re-release of the movie, which was a bigger deal in those days before home video. Still, most other sci-fi franchises (like *Star Trek*, *Star Wars*, and *Battlestar Galactica*) saw comic books produced almost immediately with the franchise's debut. Not only did the *2001* comic take almost a decade to appear, but there was no sequel film or novel, nor any other new material set in the Space Odyssey universe, during this intervening time. (The sequel novel, *2010*, wouldn't appear until 1982, and its film adaptation had to wait until 1984.)

And make no mistake – the comic was an adaptation and continuation of the Stanley Kubrick film, not the Arthur C. Clarke novel that also appeared in 1968.[1]

For another thing, the 1968 film has come to be regarded as almost sacred. Although it received mixed reviews upon its release (negative reviews pointing out the film's plodding pace and lack of conflict during its

---

[1] Kubrick and Clarke collaborated on the plot, based on a few of Arthur C. Clarke's short stories (including his 1948 "The Sentinel"). But in recognition of the film's prominence, Clarke's sequel novels were effectively sequels to the film and not his own novel. So perhaps it's no surprise that the comic takes the film as its starting point – especially since adapting novels to comics wasn't common in 1976.

first half), *2001* steadily increased in reputation and influence. Today, it's often considered one of the finest films ever made and even more universally considered one of the finest sci-fi movies in history. Making it into a comic book can seem a little like adapting and continuing *Citizen Kane*.

This pattern of reception, from mixed reviews to greater praise over time, is typical of many films directed by Stanley Kubrick. *Dr. Strangelove* (1964), *A Clockwork Orange* (1971), *The Shining* (1980), and *Full Metal Jacket* (1987) are all regarded as classic films, although they divided critics upon release. Kubrick, perhaps more than any other American director, is regarded as an auteur – a singular creative mind who dominates his work, even when it's a collaboration (as all films are). It's hard to imagine a comic-book continuation of those other films. (Perhaps featuring the further adventures of the sociopathic Alex from *Clockwork Orange*, returning to ultra-violence and "the old in-out?")

The very idea feels like sacrilege, less because of the low status afforded comics (one hopes) and more because any such continuation, by other creative minds in *any* medium, seems to dilute the special nature of the original. It's equally hard to imagine a cartoon series based on *Full Metal Jacket* (and if you don't believe this could happen, based on the violent content of that film, both *Rambo* and *RoboCop* got cartoons).

In 1976, however, Kubrick's *2001: A Space Odyssey* hadn't yet become such a sacred text. It was well-regarded enough that adapting it into one of Marvel's oversized "treasury" editions might have made sense to someone at the company. After all, there were no home videos at the time, and adaptations served the very real purpose of giving readers *some* version of a movie that they could enjoy at home. With the film's many grand visuals, it must have seemed like it was a perfect match for the treasury format – even if the film had come out almost a decade earlier. Having adapted the film, an ongoing series might have seemed to make sense to Marvel. After all, such a beautiful treasury adaptation could serve as a high-profile springboard for such a series.

Even so, it's worth noting that *Star Wars* – which sent Hollywood scrambling to approve sci-fi films – wouldn't come out until the following year (1977). Marvel had great success adapting and continuing that film.

But in 1976, there was no history of success to point to, when making the choice to adapt and continue *2001* -- a film from eight years prior.

But the *strangest* thing about Kirby's *2001* is that Jack Kirby was the one to do it.

Kubrick's *2001* is characterized by its long takes, its meditative quality, and its almost total lack of action. It's certainly a visually stunning film — perhaps that's even its strongest element. But these visuals are elegant, beautiful, and characterized by their geometric precision and, indeed, their minimalism. *Everything* is understated. Even when what's being depicted concerns the fate of humanity, the dialogue is banal — when there's dialogue at all. The music's often more important than any words, and there's certainly no punches and photon torpedoes, nor anything of the sort.

It's hard to overstate just how ill-suited Jack Kirby was to such material.

Like the film, Kirby's visual style is distinctive, but it couldn't be more different in tone. Kirby is bombastic. His art is famous for its extreme foreshortening, adding a sense of drama and excitement to leaps and punches. He's action-oriented and in-your-face, whereas Kubrick's film was all about the subtle. No one ever accused Kirby of being subtle. Indeed, his almost complete lack of subtlety is part of his charm. It's just not a charm which one could possibly imagine fitting *2001*.

The famous visuals in *2001* are stark. Minimal. Kirby's art is anything but. Indeed, while he was certainly a master of the comics form and profoundly influential, his art is often rather ugly. He excelled at wild, jagged technological devices, brimming with otherworldly energy, but his figures are all muscles, and his faces are almost uniformly brutish. His characters — yes, even the women — often look like mashed-up street brawlers, even when they're supposed to be royalty, or are supposed to be defined by their gracefulness. There's certainly an elegance to Kirby's wild illustrations, but they're not exactly *elegant*.

Many of the long shots in *2001* are about establishing a sense of *place* — whether it's feeling the ship overwhelmed by the black vastness of space, or being able to visualize how humans would interact with the ship's circular interior. Even as the ship's computer, HAL, is deactivated, one gets a sense of the size of the room and how one navigates it in zero gravity. It's because of a porthole's position that HAL is able to read the astronauts' lips and figure out their plan. These are real settings, not sci-fi backdrops.

Kirby, in contrast, almost never communicates place in this way. He would toss torches or technological devices into a scene, but their function is to communicate ambiance, not to let the reader imagine characters interacting with a real, three-dimensional space. He's simply not concerned with such matters, nor does he seem to see such precise settings as an integral part of the story itself. Even on this fairly subtle level, Kirby and Kubrick were very different brains.

Then there's Kirby's prose, which is often wildly overwritten — a pattern he learned from earlier periods in comics history, when captions could describe what was shown visually, and from his collaboration with Stan Lee specifically. This doesn't fit well with the film's long dialogue-free sequences. Kirby's prose is also spectacularly purple — more poetic than Lee's and at times quite effective, but purple nonetheless. Again, not a great fit with Kubrick. Especially when, in the comic, Kirby would use captions and thought balloons to spell out, in melodramatic language, what the film leaves implicit or ambiguous.

Kirby and Kubrick also had almost antithetical creative approaches. Kirby was famous for banging out multiple pages a day and working on several monthly titles simultaneously. He maintained a remarkable level of quality, given this level of production. But he didn't sweat the small stuff. Kubrick took years to make a single movie, and he was famous for driving his actors to madness by redoing the same scene over and over, without giving them almost anything in the way of notes or advice, simply because what he'd filmed wasn't perfect or the way he saw it in his head.

Kubrick may have been ambiguous and plodding, but he thought deeply. While filming *The Shining*, he famously (depending on which story you believe) called Stephen King in the middle of the night to confront the horror writer's beliefs about God. Kirby's work dabbled in philosophy, but it didn't probe too deeply or in any organized or sustained way. Philosophy was a *theme* to Kirby, who wasn't an intellectual.

None of this should be seen as anti-Kirby, nor pro-Kubrick. Kubrick's perfectionism abused actors, and he scrapped material that represented huge expenditures of talent and money. And what Kirby's work lacks in intellect or pristine beauty, it more than makes up for in dynamism and a vitality that seems to leap off the page. It's arguably as hard to imagine comics without Kirby as it is cinema without Kubrick.

The point isn't that either man's style is superior to the other. It's that they're so completely incompatible, so utterly at odds with one another, that it staggers the imagination that one man would be tasked to adapt and continue the work of the other.

Jack Kirby's *2001: A Space Odyssey* shouldn't work. Sometimes, such odd combinations work anyway, while creators who seem perfectly matched to their content sometimes fail. This isn't one of those exceptions. Kirby's *2001* is, instead, the most bizarre sort of failure – a crazy comic that by all rights shouldn't exist but somehow does. Like the way we'd feel about a continuation of *Citizen Kane* by Frank Miller, if one actually existed.

It's an oddity produced by a sci-fi time rift, or a product of a parallel universe. It certainly doesn't belong in ours.

And that is its greatest charm.

On Jack Kirby's *2001: A Space Odyssey* Adaptation

Before Jack Kirby continued the story of *2001*, he adapted the film into a 70-page comic.[2] Although the comic adapts the film — it uses Jupiter, for example, whereas the novel used Saturn[3] — it does incorporate some dialogue from the novel. Strangely, it also incorporates elements from the screenplay, in which the computer HAL spoke more colloquially. Such inconsistencies with the finished film are common in adaptations produced in time for the motion picture release, but they're rarer in adaptations produced long after the fact, as this one was.

The adaptation is divided into four chapters. The first follows Moonwatcher, the main ape who encounters the alien Monolith in the beginning of *2001*, thus kickstarting human evolution.

Of course, this entire sequence lacks dialogue in the film — there's no human to speak, after all, and music famously fills in the gap. In Kirby's comic, however, *every single panel* has a caption, describing what's

---

[2] The oversized comic also contained the 10-page "2001: A Space Retrospective," featuring text about the film with David Anthony Kraft, accompanied by copious photographs.
[3] Reportedly, the only reason the film didn't use Saturn was because imagining its rings on film was thought to be too expensive, so Jupiter was used instead.

The Monolith as Kirby depicts it, adapting the famous scene from the opening of *2001: A Space Odyssey*. From Kirby's 1976 adaptation. Art by Jack Kirby.

happening, what Moonwatcher thinks and feels, and telling us the significance of what we're witnessing. At times this works -- as when Kirby tells us that Moonwatcher doesn't know the ape he's found dead is his own father, since he doesn't understand reproduction. At other times, the captions feel like they're spelling things out far too much, or even preempting us from observing and thinking – a process the sequence in the film triggers rather effectively.

More startling is Kirby's depiction of the Monolith. An all-black space on the page would be hard to pull off, and Kirby can't resist depicting it more dramatically. He even includes his famous "Kirby crackle" – those overlapping dots that are supposed to look like energy, brimming over or escaping out of some device. The result looks more like something out of Kirby's *Fantastic Four* than the Kubrick film.

In the film, this initial sequence ends with a dramatic cut to 2001, as the image of a bone tossed into the air gives way to the image of a spaceship moving through space. It's a surprising juxtaposition, and not only because it jumps forward millions of years. It also implies a connection between the bone, as a primitive tool, and the eventual development of space travel. It's the natural evolution of our ability to use tools, spurred by the Monolith – or so the film seems to be communicating through this visual shorthand.

To his credit, Kirby seeks to adapt this powerful transition. But he does so in panels of different sizes, so that the bone almost seems to morph into the spaceship. It feels too literal, yet it fails to recognize that a more literal translation into comics – using (likely silent) panels of the same size, simply positioning the bone in the same position as the spacecraft in the following panel – would be more successful. Kirby's not so much adapting the famous cinematic cut into the comics form as much as adapting them into the *super-hero* comics form.

Kirby's captions also manage to miss the point of the cut. Instead of describing humanity's use of tools, he focuses on underlining his adaptation of the transition by describing the bone's trajectory in ways reminiscent of a spaceship. In the page's third and final panel, he places emphasis on the amazing shift from the distant past to the year 2001, which is the most superficial aspect of the transition – ignoring any of the sequence's philosophical implications, involving tools or evolution, that one might expect these captions to play with, if not actually tease out.

As with the Monolith, Kirby can't resist depicting outer space in his typical, flamboyant way. Instead of the mostly black void seen in the film, we now have a black and pink field that's positively filled with excitement – a purple atmosphere, two explosions (one of purple, the other orange), light blue orbs inexplicably floating copiously, and Kirby crackle *everywhere*.

None of this makes any sense, of course, but it's oh so *dramatic*. It also completely removes the realism and majestic minimalism of the original film.

In the film, the transition from prehistory to the then-future of 2001 is accomplished through a smash cut, juxtaposing a bone in flight with a spaceship. From *2001: A Space Odyssey* (1968).

10 The Weirdest Sci-Fi Comic Ever Made: Understanding Jack Kirby's *2001*

Kirby's version of the same transition. From his 1976 comics adaptation of *2001: A Space Odyssey*. Art by Jack Kirby.

As the adaptation begins its second chapter (melodramatically and not-so-inventively titled "The Thing on the Moon!"), Kirby uses the adaptation's first of many photo-collage panels. Kirby helped popularize this technique in comics earlier in the 1970s (especially on DC's *New Gods*), and there's no denying that it fits well with outer-space material – especially an adaptation of realistic sci-fi like *2001*.

Unfortunately, when juxtaposed with the previous page, it also underlines how cartoony Kirby's own depiction of space is. Kirby uses this technique throughout the adaptation, and it consistently produces this effect. But it's particularly pronounced here, in its first instance, coming immediately after the story's rather absurd first depiction of outer space.

As he continues his adaptation Kirby (to his credit) takes the time to adapt elements that depict space flight realistically, yet which serve no other real purpose. Characters and instruments defy gravity, accompanied by Kirby's captions that spell out *how* this is done, which might be foreign to the movie but not to the novel. It's the kind of thing you rarely see in sci-fi comics, where outer-space settings are usually exotic backdrops, in which characters stand and act exactly as they would on Earth – which surely represents a failure of the creative imagination, given that these conventions in TV and film are primarily due to budget considerations that comics don't have.

Also to his credit, Kirby adapts the long journey to the Monolith on the moon, which doesn't feature much conflict and isn't exactly Kirby's métier. Here, Kirby faces a challenge: rendering some rather talky and expository material into the visual comics form. Of course, cinema is also visual, but it's limited in that it doesn't change its aspect ratio, so almost all shots are of the same size, barring the rare use of the split-screen technique or cropping an image so that it's not the full screen size. Comics, of course, are constrained by the size of the page in a similar way, but most comics don't feature a single panel per page. Instead, comics break that space into static panels, and the size and placement of each panel can reflect the *contents* of the panel. In this way, the *shape* of the image can be used to control the pace, to emphasize, and to give room to visuals deserving of this attention – whereas cinema tends to give the same *space* to someone talking as it does a magnificent vista. Kirby, a natural at manipulating these elements of the comics form, uses these advantages over the material's source medium.

For example, when the Monolith is revealed – but not shown – during a presentation, Kirby uses a large panel to show the audience's various shocked reactions. He can't resist heightening the melodrama, with a caption and various word balloons, whereas a more understated large panel would probably work better – although this would have gone counter to the way comics were produced at the time, especially in Kirby's more mainstream circles. Nonetheless, he knows to follow the smaller expository panels with this larger one, and it's the *size* of the panel that emphasizes the melodrama, more than Kirby's dialogue or captions.

An even better example occurs when the protagonists are en route to the Monolith on the Moon. The comics page, like the cinema screen, seems invariable in size, even broken up into multiple panels or split-screen images. But of course, the comics page *isn't* invariable in size. Comics can *double* that size at any time by simply continuing art from one page to the next. Comics have even included fold-out pages to get even *more* size. Today, online comes aren't limited to any consistent "page" size at all. For cinema to do such a thing, it would have to expand the size of the movie or TV screen. Kirby exploits this strength of the comics medium, relative to film, by employing a double-page spread, adding visual drama to a sequence that's devoid of action. And this looks even better in the large, tabloid-size format, in which this adaptation was published.

When the characters visit the excavation pit where the Monolith stands, Kirby mirrors the film quite closely. The biggest difference is how he depicts outer space as an area of wild activity, rather than a deadly black field. As a result, the image appears less stark and indisputably less realistic – but here, Kirby's expressive outer space horizon makes the image, and thus the Monolith, seem even more alien, even more bizarre.

Kirby's depiction of the black Monolith itself, like the blackness of space, shares the same wild expressionism. Like Kirby's ancient Monolith at the beginning of the story, the Monolith on the Moon is brimming with energy. In the film, it's a black void like space itself – cool, dispassionate, featureless, and more frightening for it. Perhaps this wouldn't translate well into comics, but it feels like Kirby can't resist transforming the Monolith into

Astronauts approach the excavation pit on the Moon where a Monolith has been unearthed, as seen in the 1968 film (top) and in Jack Kirby's 1976 comics adaptation. Despite the similarity of the composition, note the very different way in which Kirby depicts the space above the horizon.

a piece of alien technology that emits wild swirls of energy – not unlike the super-hero technology he spent much of his career drawing, or the way Kirby finds outer space more interesting when it looks more like a Pop Art version of an expressionist painting than anything human or recognizable. The result is a Monolith that's more certainly more viscerally *exciting* than the film's but in a pulpy way bearing almost no relationship to the film's austere cerebralism.

As Kirby shifts to the story's third chapter, he tries to echo the film's moving images, much as he did in the transition from the first to the second chapter. Here, he uses four page-wide panels of the same size to depict the movement of the Discovery One through space, on its way to Jupiter, echoing the long shots of the same in Kubrick's film. It's a good idea, and Kirby is wise to use panels of the same size, echoing the static size of the cinema screen (which he failed to do in the earlier chapter transition). But Kirby can't resist adding captions, which use many words without either propelling the plot forward or poetically teasing out implications of what we're seeing. And here, Kirby's expressionistic depiction of space radically undermines what he's depicting. He's adapted a scene that's about the tedium and isolation of what real-life space travel might be like, but he's set this sequence not in space at all but in some bizarre otherworldly dimension.

This isn't outer space. It's more like the Negative Zone of Kirby's *Fantastic Four*. It's certainly not our solar system, nor any space we might recognize.

Chapter three (which Kirby titles "Ahead Lie the Planets") contains the material that's probably the most frequently referenced portion of the film: the conflict with HAL on board the Discovery One.

Here again, Kirby echoes the film's visuals closely. When these visuals are on board the ship, they don't suffer from the problems inherent with Kirby's depiction of space, nor his energetic portrayal of fantastic technology like the Monolith.

One of the most successful pages in the entire adaptation is of the centrifugal room from the film, in which Frank Poole goes jogging. Here, Kirby takes full advantage of the fact that the comics "screen" is of variable

On Jack Kirby's 2001: A Space Odyssey Adaptation   15

Jack Kirby uses the variable shape of panels to successfully adapt the centrifugal interior of the Discovery One. From his 1976 comics adaptation of *2001: A Space Odyssey*. Art by Jack Kirby.

dimensions, employing panels as tall as the page to emphasize the verticality of the image, in which there's no up or down.

That's something Kubrick couldn't do in *2001*, with a screen inflexibly wider than it is tall. Indeed, watching the film, it's easy to wish the dimensions of the film were more vertical, and Kubrick has to wrestle against the medium of cinema itself in these scenes.

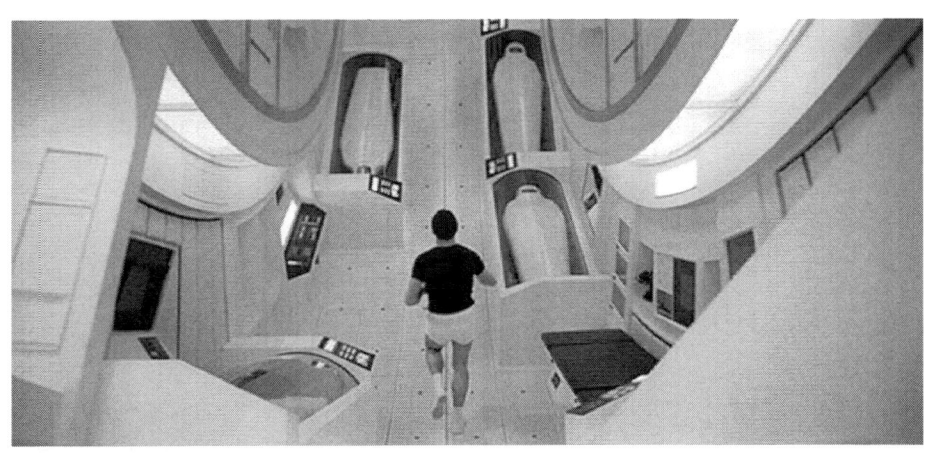

The same jogging sequence, as seen in the 1968 film.

Playing with the shapes of panels might seem obvious, but Kirby employs this strength of the comics medium brilliantly – especially given the added height of the tabloid format. Here, at least, Kirby's arguably *improved* upon the original – and used the strengths of the comics medium to do so.

On the other hand, Kirby fails rather completely in adapting the famous scene in which HAL reads the astronauts' lips, foiling their attempt to avoid HAL from overhearing. In the film, Kubrick gets the viewer to understand what's happening by focusing on the HAL console, then depicting the astronauts from his perspective and closing in on their talking – but silent – lips. In this, the film communicates what's happening through a series of juxtaposed images, first causing us to understand that we're seeing things from HAL's perspective and then causing us to focus on the astronaut's lips.

It's fully possible to reproduce all of this in comics, although it would take several panels to do so, since the effect requires the juxtaposition of multiple images. To make sure the effect was communicated, several panels could zoom in on the astronaut's lips. And given Kirby's predilection for captions, any ambiguity in the sequence could be spelled out so as to make what's happening perfectly clear for readers.

Instead, Kirby just handles all of this in a single panel. He simply uses a caption to tell us that HAL's reading lips. The panel's image is itself quite close to the original, but the *effect* couldn't be more different.

It's certainly... an *economical* solution. But it's not very successful, subtle, or imaginative. It uses one of the strengths of comics – the written word – as a way of *avoiding* solving a problem in adapting visual narrative. Instead of using writing as a separate "track," not unlike sound in film, capable of accenting or undercutting the visual "track," Kirby's used it here to avoid coming up with a visual solution, or taking the space necessary to do so.

If Kirby's depiction of the centrifugal chamber represents some of the *best* of comics, this panel represents some of the *worst*.

Of course, it's not like Kirby was alone in using captions to "fix" visual problems and narrative ambiguities. Stan Lee did so *all the time*. Silver Age Marvel comics are filled with this kind of incredibly poor storytelling (such as characters tossing something not previously shown, with only a caption explaining how they got it, or even *why* they're doing what they're doing). In Kirby's defense, he's only repeating the bad habits he learned from a long career in corporate comics.

Kirby's more successful at other points in this chapter, and he seems to thrive on the conflict in this section of the film. He's also not immune to granting space to sequences he finds interesting, even if he didn't feel inclined to do so with the lip-reading sequence. When HAL kills Frank Poole, Kirby depicts the astronaut's body adrift over three panels – much like he did with the Discovery One, upon its introduction. And later, when Dave Bowman reenters the ship, Kirby gives the image of the tumbling astronaut a full splash page – it's just the kind of thing Kirby's art excels at.

Of course, Kirby adds captions and thought balloons, which either add little or spell things out a bit too much. For example, when Dave Bowman goes to check on the astronauts in suspended animation, Kirby has Bowman think, "Let me be *wrong!* Let my *suspicions* be groundless – above all – let me be in *time!*" It's the kind of thought balloon that would be at home in Silver Age Marvel comics, but it has no place in an adaptation of *2001*.

More successful is the sequence in which Bowman deactivates HAL. Here, Kirby doesn't have the benefit of audio, so HAL's dispassionate tone of voice, his vocal degeneration, and his singing of "Daisy" is impossible to fully represent on the silent comics page. But Kirby's able to represent the sequence over multiple panels of varying size, depicting the sequence from multiple points of view – most dramatically in a splash page that exploits the adaptation's oversized format. What the sequence lacks in detail, it makes up for in its sense of expansiveness. It's not nearly as successful *overall* as the film's version, but it does have some advantages over the original.

With the Discovery One no longer able to sustain life, Dave Bowman abandons it in a pod, occasioning another photo-collage page. Drifting in space over Jupiter, Bowman encounters another Monolith – which Kirby can't resist depicting in a splash page that manages to combine his wildly expressive depiction of outer space with his depiction of the Monoliths as crackling with energy. It's his most over-the-top page of the adaptation yet – so much so that, taken on its own and out of context, it would be almost impossible to tell even what it depicts.

This leads into the fourth and final chapter, colorfully titled "The Dimension Trip!" In the film, this segment is famous for its long symbolic sequence (sometimes called the "stargate" sequence), which attempts to represent an ambiguous transcendence in cinematic form. Kirby's adaptation feels much shorter – but it's no less abstract. In trying to represent the awesomeness of the experience, Kirby incorporates *two* double-page splashes into the sequence.

It's a smart choice, even if Kirby's visuals surprisingly don't seem to capture the majesty of the cinematic sequence. Despite not being constrained by budget considerations, Kirby's imagery here simply isn't that imaginative.

Here again, the adaptation seems to willfully literalize what's depicted. In the film, once the vision starts, Dave Bowman and the pod disappear, and the viewer is immersed in what we presume Bowman is experiencing. The vision takes over the film, and in this way the experience is made subjective.

In Kirby's version, we see Bowman's floating pod amid the wild visuals, as if they're objectively happening.

Kirby seems to want the depiction to be trippy – his captions, as well as the chapter's title, certainly suggest so. But they seem far more mundane, and readers far more distant from Bowman's experience, than what we see in the film.

In the film, this gives way to a mostly white room, in the Louis XVI style, and it's not at all clear that this is a physical place at all. Indeed, given the subjectivity of the visions that preceded it, the room feels like it's also a vision – like it's a representation of the austere, rational calm at the center of the chaos of the mind, not unlike the eye of a hurricane.

In Kirby's version, the caption that begins this portion of the story explicitly tells us "the Monolith has [...] remove[d] Bowman's pod to its own *special* place..." The setting, we're told, is a *physical* place – not a symbolic mental one. Here again, the story is literalized precisely where the film thrived on ambiguity.

David Bowman finds himself in the Louis XVI style. From Jack Kirby's 1976 comics adaptation of *2001: A Space Odyssey*. Art by Jack Kirby.

If Kirby seems uniquely ill-suited to the minimal aesthetic of Kubrick's *2001*, it's here that this clash seems the most apparent. It's hard to imagine anything more outside of Kirby's comfort zone than an extended sequence taking place in almost colorless Louis XVI rooms. One marvels at what Kirby must have thought about tackling such a sequence – although, as such a versatile workhorse, he may have simply powered through. Still, there's arguably nothing so strange in the whole of the adaptation, which is so defined by Kirby's aesthetic, as seeing him illustrate this particular sequence, which is so defined by tactile concerns and bound up in the effect of their careful observation.

In these environs, Bowman ages unto death. In the film, this aging occurs in stages, and the transitions from one age to another occur as Bowman sees his older self, which then takes over as protagonist and focus. Of course, these transitions are visually interesting, but they raise questions of identity: are we following the *same* Bowman, only older and displaced in time, or different versions of David Bowman? This helps to emphasize the subjectivity of the sequence, in which it's not at all clear what's literally happening.

But as we've seen, Kirby's adaptation repeatedly literalizes the story, lessening its ambiguity. For example, the captions describe this setting as a physical place, which isn't clear in the film – where it could be, for example, a virtual construction within the Monument itself. So it shouldn't surprise us that Kirby leaves out these transitions between stages of Bowman's aging.

Kirby goes further in this literalization, suggesting that not only is this a physical place but one where Bowman's every need is provided for him. Because of this, the sequence feels less like a subjective vision than a kind of alien zoo, in which Bowman is kept by the Monolith. The captions do underline the fuzziness of Bowman's perceptions and memories of this place, but it remains a *physical* place, in which physical laws seem to apply. For example, Bowman seems to *need* to eat in Kirby's version, whereas in the film it feels more as if he eats simply because he *thinks* he must or is used to doing so. The two versions aren't utterly incompatible, but the film's is far more mental and subjective, while Kirby's is -- true to his personal tendencies – far more physical and "real."

Kirby also spells out *why* this sequence is happening at all – at least in superficial terms. A caption tells us that "the old one must pass before the *new one* can come into being..." This is, of course, *symbolically* true in the film, in which Bowman ages and dies over this sequence, before attaining some sort of cosmic consciousness – or a consciousness as advanced, relative to our own, as we are to the apes at the beginning of the film. But there's a vast difference between what's *symbolically* true (and perhaps *feels* right to the audience) and what's *literally* true. In the film, this entire sequence could be simply a mental way station, what happens to Bowman's mind on the edge of this new consciousness, as he sheds his former self. Equally, the sequence could be the Monolith deliberately preparing Bowman for what comes next. It's up to us, as readers, to navigate these possibilities. Kirby's captions preempt this. They're not *wrong*; it's just that, in underlining *one* possibility, they close off others.

David Bowman encounters the Monolith as he dies. From Jack Kirby's 1976 comics adaptation of *2001: A Space Odyssey*. Art by Jack Kirby.

Of course, Bowman dies, and he's transformed into a new, more advanced being. In the film, this is represented by the image of a baby against the cosmos. Whether this is a physical representation or not isn't clear in the film. Such questions, we may realize, have by this point long been abandoned by the film. The "star child" image (as it's come to be known) is certainly symbolic, however, of a new birth, suggesting the beginning of a new stage in human evolution, in which our species might adjust to its new, outer-space environment, and in which it might interact meaningfully with alien intelligences.

Unsurprisingly, all of this is literalized in Kirby's adaptation, in which Bowman seems to physically be in this place – and seems to *physically* be transformed into some sort of a cosmic baby.

Kirby also describes what this cosmic baby goes on to do: to wander "the universe" (not the galaxy or "the stars" but the universe) until it finds a planet it likes, which it will then inhabit.

In the film, it's implicit that Bowman's new "form" – if indeed it is a physical form – represents a new stage in human evolution, parallel to how the Monolith triggered a leap in human consciousness near the beginning of the film. But this is only gestured at. Obviously, David Bowman isn't among a community of humans, like the apes were in the beginning. We assume that this new stage in human evolution will take place among the stars, which are home to extraterrestrial intelligences that our minds can barely process – hence the ambiguity and symbolism of the film's ending. But what this new stage in human evolution will look like is anybody's guess – if we are even capable of understanding it.

Kirby's adaptation tells us that Bowman has been literally and physically transformed into a kind of cosmic baby. Kirby's adaptation tells us what that baby will do: wander "the universe" and find a new planet to inhabit – though this doesn't really help much, since we don't know *what* it seeks to do on such a planet. But Kirby's adaptation also tells us that Bowman is "the *first* of *many*. For the Monolith knows there must be *more* than one new seed to sow the harvest of a new species…"

In the film, because Bowman's alone when he's "transformed," it's not clear how or if this represents a new stage for humanity as a whole. His destiny may well be humanity's overall destiny, but it's not at all clear how the rest of humanity will get there — or if this is indeed the Monolith's intent. For all we know, the Monolith is simply elevating Bowman and leaving humanity to find its own way. It's at this point that the parallels between the Monolith's actions in the beginning of the film and the Monolith's actions at the end break down.

While this is ambiguous — and perhaps appropriately so, given the idea that we, as current humans, could not understand this alien intelligence — it's also one of the film's weakest points. The problem isn't ambiguity itself, but rather a matter of the film following through on its own structure. The evolutionary boost the Monolith gave humanity in the beginning is supposed to mirror the Monolith's transformation of David Bowman at the end. Indeed, without this mirroring, we couldn't understand that later transformation. Ambiguity can be wonderful — and appropriate, especially in depicting the unfathomably alien. But when a parallel that a text itself establishes doesn't really seem to work, praising ambiguity can be a way of hiding an inherent structural flaw — or at least a lack of completeness. Ambiguity isn't its own reward. And *2001* is lopsided in this way: is Bowman's elevation at the end the next stage of human evolution, parallel to the beginning, or is it just something that happens to the final survivor of a doomed spaceship?

Any adaptation must *adapt* — and thus change — the original. Ideally, these changes make the result work better, not only in a new medium but also in terms of its narrative. Adaptations often fix ambiguities, where ambiguities weren't intended and don't help a story. Kirby's adaptation may be wrongheaded in several respects, especially in its literalization of things the film is wise to leave ambiguous. But here at least, the way Kirby tends to spell things out may be seen as improving upon the original. If the film's ending mirrors its beginning — and only makes sense, to the extent it does, because of this — why is Bowman alone, whereas the apes evolved as part of a society?

Kirby's answer is simplistic: Bowman is just the first. It's not a bad answer, and it's perfectly consistent with the film. There's certainly nothing in the film to contradict this. And it does sort of solve a structural problem with the film, in which the ending seems to mirror the beginning but doesn't, really.

Of course, this benefits Kirby's agenda, because it sets up his own ongoing series, in which we'll follow the Monolith's program to elevate humanity. It's hard to figure out where to go next, after the transcendental ending of *2001*, and Kirby's figured out one way of doing so — a way that, while not subtle, does address one of the problems inherent in the original.

Jack Kirby's *2001: A Space Odyssey* Continuation, Part 1

Kirby's continuation of *2001* is nothing short of flabbergasting.

It shouldn't exist.

It's so odd, so *wrong*, that it loops back around upon itself — not all the way back to being *right*, for sure, but to be charming for its sheer impossible-to-make-up oddity.

Kirby's ongoing *2001*, following his treasury-sized adaptation of the film, lasted only ten issues. Of these, the first four issues and the final six issues were very different.

Prehistory and Future: The First Four Issues

All three stories in the first four issues followed the same formula.

2001, A Space Odyssey #1 (Dec 1976) — yes, the comics title used a comma instead of a colon — opens with a splash page featuring a caveman with a Monolith behind him. The imagery and language is immediately identifiable as Kirby, and it seems radically out of step with the *2001* we know. The captions on the first page end by referring to the Monolith: "Read on -- and behold its awesome secrets!" Few things could seem less like Kubrick's film than this.

26   The Weirdest Sci-Fi Comic Ever Made: Understanding Jack Kirby's *2001*

Readers approaching the comic today (especially those familiar with Arthur C. Clarke's own sequels) might well expect any continuation to take place largely in space, perhaps on the Moon or around Jupiter. Instead, we're treated to the story of Beast-Killer, a caveman in what is today New Orleans, who battles other cavemen and has a connection to the Monolith. He battles a saber-toothed tiger, then fashions the first spear. As he throws it, the story transitions to outer space through a juxtaposition of an astronaut in the same posture — a transition echoing the famous bone / spaceship smash cut in *2001* (which Kirby preserved in his adaptation).

Jack Kirby transitions from prehistory to the then-future 2001, echoing the film's similar transition through juxtaposition. From *2001, A Space Odyssey* #1 (Dec 1976). Art by Jack Kirby and Mike Royer.

At this point, the issue's already halfway done. Kirby's echoing the beginning of *2001* by imagining that what we saw there was only one of several such interventions by the Monolith. That's not inconsistent with *2001*, but it's still a strange idea. Did Kirby think fans of *2001* wanted more apes and cavemen? Or that this was the heart of the story? It's as if he's confusing a story's prologue with the meat of the story.

Woodrow Decker, the astronaut in question, is one of two who are stranded on an asteroid in the asteroid belt between Mars and Jupiter. And this particular asteroid is filled with ruins of some sort of ancient civilization. In *2001*, the voyage to Jupiter was a big deal, and there's no evidence that humans have explored the asteroid belt. Kirby gives no indication that these ruins were made by the same aliens that built the Monolith – the idea seems to be that the Monoliths of *2001* represent aliens having left things behind in our solar system, so why not have more odd stuff left behind?

To a fan of *2001*, this ought to seem strange indeed, because *2001* was very controlled in its depiction of the Monoliths, and their discovery means a great deal. Suddenly, in Kirby's very first issue, alien artifacts in our solar system can be casually inserted into a plot, without any need to explain who left them or why.

One can almost guess at Kirby's thinking here: "Hey, did *2001* really explain the Monolith? *2001* fans don't want explanations. They just want more alien artifacts and ruins."

The two astronauts' spaceship is burning. On an asteroid, which clearly doesn't have an atmosphere, or the astronauts wouldn't be wearing spacesuits. So where's the fire getting the oxygen to burn? It's a tiny objection, to be sure, but it's a complete violation of the careful realism that defined *2001*'s depiction of space travel.

The astronauts descend into an underground alien building – where they're attacked by a tentacled purple space monster with big yellow eyes. No, really. It's hiding in the ruins on the asteroid. And no, it doesn't need a spacesuit.

This may be classic Kirby fare, but it's impossible to imagine Kubrick or Clarke casually inserting such a beast onto an asteroid, let alone casually inserting alien ruins for the monster to inhabit.

At this point, anyone who's seen *2001* ought to be asking what the fuck they're reading. And what the fuck Kirby was thinking.

It's as if he's turned *2001* into a Kirby space adventure comic.

After one of the astronauts is killed, Woodrow Decker, now the sole survivor – and a descendant, we're told, of Beast-Killer, the caveman from the issue's first half – discovers a Monolith deep inside the ruins. He dives into it — as if it's one of the comic-book portals Kirby spent his career drawing, despite such a maneuver not having been shown in *2001*.

At this point, Kirby turns to the stargate sequence from the film, although a bit different for Woodrow Decker than it was in the film for David Bowman. Kirby excels here, letting himself go wild with the visuals. Instead of Decker seeing wild imagery, like Bowman did in *2001*, Decker visits "world upon world," including an encounter with a mammoth green alien.

And then Decker is in a wooded area, much as Bowman famously found himself in white Louis XVI rooms. Like Bowman, Decker quickly ages and dies in this new setting, whereupon he's received and transformed by the Monolith.

As in Kirby's adaptation of the film, Decker is *literally* transformed into a cosmic baby, which then goes flying off through the cosmos. This isn't at all clear in the film itself, but it's part of Kirby's rather literal adaptation, so he repeats it here.

And that's the end of the issue. Incredibly, the next issue promises "Vira the She-Demon!"

Not a continuation of Decker's story, mind you. Nor Bowman the cosmic baby meeting up with Woodrow Decker the cosmic baby. Nor an update about what's happening with humanity as a whole, or on the Moon after *2001*, or something involving Discovery One dead over Jupiter.

No, "Vira the She-Demon!" In a *2001* comic.

HAL 9000, meet Vira the She-Demon. The two of you shouldn't exist in the same world together, but now you do.

Corporate American comics, in which Jack Kirby had worked most of his life, routinely combine genres that really shouldn't go together. Thus, a hard-boiled detective comic can share the same universe with an alien invasion comic — even though the insertion of aliens into the universe of the hard-boiled detective effectively destroys the realistic ambiance on which that detective depends. In the same way, characters relying on magic mix with realistic science-fiction characters, despite that the insertion of magic into realistic science fiction transforms that genre into something closer to science *fantasy*. Control over genre — and with it tone — is crucial to any story, and the more realistic genre typically suffers when unrealistic characters or elements are introduced. Popeye may be great, and *The Great Gatsby* may be too, but the latter's universe is shattered by Popeye's insertion. Corporate American comics don't usually know, or at least care, about this dynamic. But literary works, whether in prose or film or comics, typically care a great deal about this careful control of genre, tone, and realism.

That's true of *2001*, which Kubrick made sure was as realistic as possible, even when it was painful and costly to shoot. Everything was controlled.

Such control is foreign to Kirby, who spent his career in corporate comics, where the most realistic characters can meet funny anthropomorphic animals. Kubrick's careful literary control was foreign to Kirby, who excelled at producing wild comics stories at a breakneck pace.

And so we get alien ruins on an asteroid, a spaceship burning in space, and Vira the She-Demon.

It's hard to find words to adequately express how strange all of this is. The comic couldn't feel more out of sync with *2001*. It's all Kirby, no Kubrick or Clarke. It's mind-boggling. It's just not right.

It seems as if Kirby sees the central story of *2001* as "Monolith intervenes to spur human evolution; then in 2001, a future human in space encounters a Monolith and gets turned into a cosmic baby." Kirby's strategy, in continuing this story, seems to be to repeat this formula, as if the Monolith is assembling some sort of cosmic baby super-team.

It's as if Kirby looked at *2001* and saw the Monolith as a *deus ex machina* – a plot contrivance that could be used to justify almost anything. For Kirby, the Monolith is a device through which he tells wild, though ultimately formulaic, stories about both prehistoric humans and sci-fi ones, all with his classic, exaggerated flair.

If we look ahead to issue #2 (Jan 1977), we see that Vira the She-Demon will play the ape / caveman role, encountering the Monolith before the story transitions to the future to show a descendant transfigured like David Bowman, or Woodrow Decker in Kirby's first issue.

Vira is presented with the same bombast with which Kirby presented Beast-Killer in issue #1. Her great distinguishing feature is that she's a cave*woman*, not a cave*man*. Kirby even calls her "a non-submissive female"

– language that probably wouldn't be used today. (Oh, do you mean "dominant female?")

Vira the She-Demon is clearly a riff on the cavewoman archetype, most directly riffing on Mavel's Shanna the She-Devil (who debuted a few years prior, in *Shanna the She-Devil* #1, Dec 1972). *2001* was also published by Marvel, so it's not clear why Kirby would create such an obvious analogue. In any case, neither Vira nor Shanna seem to belong in a *2001* comic.

After an encounter with the Monolith, Vira finds herself able to command the cavemen who had previously menaced her, and she sets herself up as a living goddess of sorts, with the men now delivering offerings to her instead of threats. Because these prehistoric sequences are supposed to show how the Monolith steered human evolution, we're told that the absurd stone house the men build for Vira is "perhaps the first man-made house in existence."

Is Kirby offering a metaphor for the theory that civilization was once more female-focused, before men discovered their role in reproduction? Certainly, female worship is tied here to human evolution. But the metaphor is only implicit, and one gets the sense that it's more an accident of Kirby wanting to use a cavewoman archetype, rather than having any deeper agenda.

The transition to the future is again accomplished by a visual juxtaposition. Now we're following Vera Gentry, a female astronaut with a station on Ganymede -- and a mission to investigate U.F.O. sightings there.

(Note that this is the first time Kirby gave the prehistoric protagonist and the future protagonist a similar name. In issue #1, we're only told that Beast-Killer and Woodrow Decker are related. With issue #2, Kirby began to underline the connection between the story's two disparate protagonists by making their names similar. It's a device Kirby would reuse in issues #3-4.)

If casually placing humans in the asteroid belt in issue #1 was problematic, Ganymede's even more of a problem. It's a Jovian moon, after all. Remember what a big deal going to Jupiter was, in *2001*? Now, that journey's such an unremarkable chore that Vera can complain that she's been sent at all – which she attributes to sexism, since this is such an irrelevant mission.

Jack Kirby's 2001: A Space Odyssey Continuation, Part 1   31

Jack Kirby again transitions from prehistory to the then-future 2001 through juxtaposition. From *2001, A Space Odyssey* #2 (Jan 1977). Art by Jack Kirby and Mike Royer.

If humans are now so casual about travel to Jupiter, have they investigated what happened to the Discovery One at the end of *2001*? If they have, there's no mention of it. (Such a mission would be the subject or Arthur C. Clarke's *2010: Odyssey Two*, but the need to send such a mission — or what a grand undertaking it would represent — is utterly ignored by Kirby.)

As with the alien ruins in issue #1, the fact that U.F.O.s have been spotted around Ganymede is treated like it's not at all a big deal at all to humanity. The Monoliths of *2001*, in which they eerily represented evidence of extraterrestrial visitation of our solar system, have now been reduced to one of many, many such visitations. Why, our solar system is positively teeming with alien life.

And forget the movie's careful realism, with regards to its depiction of technology. Among Vera's tools on Ganymede is what looks like a human-sized pair of binoculars. *Not a telescope. Binoculars.*

Of course, those U.F.O.s almost immediately show up – and attack without warning! Vera, alone on Ganymede, flees – only to confront green aliens in spacesuits, still attacking with no explanation!

Naturally, a Monolith saves Vera Gentry from certain death – as it saved Bowman and Decker before. A trippy sequence follows, and then Vera finds herself back home – where she has access to a swimming pool, allowing us to see her in a swimsuit. Of course, it's all been prepared by the Monolith, and Vera ages, dies, and gets transformed by the Monolith into a space baby, who then wanders the stars.

No, really. This is what Kirby's continuation, at least initially, was all about. This is the formula he took from *2001*: prehistoric adventure, future adventure, then turn into a space baby.

This has to be one of the strangest comics ever made.

In the film, it's not clear how long Bowman lives within those white Louis XVI rooms – or even if time is relevant anymore. Here, Kirby's caption tells us that Vera Gentry lives out her entire "life span" in "ninety minutes." This is making things clear where those things work precisely *because* they're ambiguous. But it also raises the question as to what possible purpose the Monolith would have in accelerating humans' aging process. That's not exactly at *odds* with the film – it's one possible interpretation. And maybe the film doesn't truly make sense either. It certainly thrives on ambiguity. But pinning this down, especially in the rudimentary way Kirby does, strips the original of its resonance and inevitably raises logical questions, which the ambiguity of the original kept us from asking.

If there was any doubt, the end of the second issue makes it clear that Kirby's formula isn't going to change soon. The blurb advertising the next issue promises to tell the story of Marak, "the barbarian's barbarian!!"

Have I mentioned this is a continuation of *2001: A Space Odyssey*?

Issues #3-4 (Feb-Mar 1977) did change things up a little – but only by expanding the tale, which still follows the same formula, although now over two issues, instead of cramming two time periods into one.

The first issue takes place entirely in prehistory, although it's thoroughly anachronistic – even by Kirby's standards. In one of his conquests, the warlord Marak meets an old man named Egel, who has encountered the Monolith and consequently has learned how to meld metal – in 200,000 B.C., long before humans had this technology. Marak follows Egel to the Monolith, where Marak has a brief vision of the far future before seeing a woman named Jalessa, who challenges him to find her. Using Egel as a kind of Hephaestus, Marak is soon outfitted in Roman-era armor, with metal swords and shields.

In issue #3's conclusion, Marak tosses the round top of a stone cask, which rolls like a wheel – a fact only Egel's inventive brain notices. Yes, this is really supposed to be the invention of the wheel.

In issue #4, Marak continues his rampage in search of Jalessa – only he now has chariots to help him. (Yes, in 200,000 B.C.)

We soon meet Jalessa, who has a stone pit with her *own* Monolith inside it. (Boy, there seem to be a lot of these things!)

Jalessa raises her private Monolith from a stone pit. From *2001, A Space Odyssey* #2 (Jan 1977). Art by Jack Kirby and Mike Royer.

The idea that the Monolith might be incorporated into ancient religion, or used in soothsaying rituals, is an exciting one that could easy serve as the starting point for a story unto itself. But here, it's only one, easily-forgotten element in a wild barbarian tale.

And just what is the Monoliths' agenda, in all of these appearances? Theoretically, they should be spurring human evolution and development. Instead, they're giving people visions and iron-working skills, long before they actually show up in history. Rather than *revealing* the mysteries of human history, Kirby's Monoliths are now blithely *violating* it. Again, Kirby seems to see the devices as little more than a *deus ex machina* that can be used to spur any sort of story he wishes to tell.

The Marak story ends when Marak is united with Jalessa. Instead of fighting, they unite peacefully — and presumably romantically. Now, Kirby's got the Monolith playing matchmaker.

The transition to the future, by way of visual juxtaposition, comes halfway through issue #4. It's a fine transition, but Kirby's own interest is clearly more in the rather incoherent barbarian tale than in what's essentially a denouement set in the far future.

The setting is a space station in orbit around Mars. Like the two futuristic settings Kirby has introduced previously, this makes no sense because it represents a major human excursion beyond the Moon, the likes of which are completely absent from *2001*.

Here too does Kirby ignore *2001*'s realism. A slew of meteors are slamming into the space station, prompting its evacuation. It's hard to imagine a swarm of meteors, packed so tightly and happening to hit a space station, which is a relatively small target in the vastness of space. This is the kind of sci-fi cliché Kubrick took pains to avoid, but if Kirby knows it's a cliché, the work gives no indication.

With the station evacuated, Commander Herb Marik remains aboard, prepared to go down with the ship, as it were. And then — surprise! — a Monolith shows up outside the space station. Marik, in an absurdly colored spacesuit, spontaneously decides to go outside to investigate!

Of course, Marik touches the Monolith, which saves him from certain death, sending him on a trippy journey through what seem like parallel dimensions — as Kirby has chosen to interpret the "stargate" sequence from

Jack Kirby again transitions from prehistory to the then-future 2001 through juxtaposition. From *2001, A Space Odyssey* #4 (Mar 1977). Art by Jack Kirby and Mike Royer.

the end of the film. Then, Marik is deposited into a mythological haven, which looks very Greco-Roman. He seems to recognize it from his dreams, and he's greeted by a woman — apparently his lover.

Unlike the end of Bowman's vision in the film, Kirby's versions are frequently populated with other people. And lest there be any confusion, Kirby's captions explain that the Monolith "has woven an environment from Marik's own dreams and placed him in it." So much for ambiguity.

But there's a twist: Marik doesn't "respond to the aging speed-process" (which, as we've noted, is only an interpretation of the film, not something necessarily *in* it). Because of this, Marik will age normally and die an old man – without being transformed into what Kirby has all along called a "new seed."

Does this represent a utopian ending for Marik (and symbolically for Marak the barbarian, whom Kirby lavished more than a full issue upon) – allowed to live his life in this heaven crafted for him? It feels like it. But why wouldn't the Monolith, which seems rather more impartial in the film, simply turn off Marik's dreamlike world, once it ascertains the man can't be transformed? And what does it mean that the Monolith has apparently failed? Why wouldn't the aging process work on Marik?

None of these questions are answered, nor is Kirby apparently interested in answering in them – despite his literalism, which has pinned down so many elements the film deliberately left ambiguous.

For our purposes, it's more important to note that the failure of Marik's transformation represents a change to Kirby's formula for the series – a formula that he would change much more radically, beginning with the next issue.

Lest we feel bad that we don't end the story with a flying space baby, Kirby gives us one anyway – although it's clear from the captions that this isn't Marik, but some other (or perhaps symbolic) star child.

And that's it. Four issues into Kirby's continuation of Kubrick's *2001*. Which collectively are almost as long as Kirby's adaptation of the film.

Who in the world thought this was what fans of *2001* wanted to see?

What was Kirby thinking?

Kirby certainly was no stranger to barbarian stories, which is really what the prehistoric sections of his *2001* stories are. He had already created *Kamandi* at DC, starring a young man in an apocalyptic future clearly riffing off *Planet of the Apes*. Shortly after his *2001*, Kirby would create *Devil Dinosaur* (#1, Apr 1978), also for Marvel. Later, after leaving Marvel (again), Kirby would work on the animated *Thundarr the Barbarian*. So perhaps he simply wanted to work on such stories, and used the opening sequence in *2001* as his justification.

Still – and in all fairness – Kirby seems to have understood little of the film. And even his science-fiction sequences, filled with unexplained aliens and human space explorers, bear no resemblance to anything in the film.

To be fair, Kirby would break the formula of his first four issues, beginning with issue #5. But his stories wouldn't become any more controlled. Nor would they feel any more in sync with the film.

This suggests the most telling insight into Kirby's mind. He seems to think that what people liked about *2001* – or at least what *he* liked about the film – was seeing an alien artifact intervene in an exotic, prehistoric setting... combined with the wild idea of future humans encountering a similar alien artifact and being transformed into some kind of super-being. One can see how such a wild hodgepodge would appeal to Kirby. But it's not *2001*.

Except that it really is. Sure, Kirby depicts both the prehistoric sequences and the future sequences through genre tropes. He's at home with stereotypical cavemen and astronauts in wild extraterrestrial settings, which are their own reward and require little explanation. But that's grafted onto a portion of the story that, while adapted, *does come from the original*.

What Kirby seems to think was essential to *2001* might seem radically misjudged. But it's material that is, after all, in *2001*.

And contrasting this with Clarke's own – later, and very different – continuation is incredibly telling, not only about Kirby and Clarke but about the tensions within *2001* itself.

Jack Kirby Vs. Arthur C. Clarke: A Tale of Two *2001* Continuations

Kirby's continuation of *2001: A Space Odyssey* takes a very different approach than Arthur C. Clarke's novels, the first of which (*2010: Odyssey Two*) appeared in 1982 and was adapted into a 1984 film. Today, far more people have seen this cinematic sequel, or read Clarke's sequel novels, than have read Kirby's (1976-1977) comic-book continuation, which could hardly be more different. But of course, Kirby's continuation came first, so it fell to him to figure out how to do so without Clarke's example to guide him.

Just as Kirby's adaptation of *2001* can help to reveal the original through contrast, so too can Clarke's continuations help us to understand Kirby's.

In *2010*, humans send a ship – the Leonov – to Jupiter to investigate what went wrong with the Discovery's 2001 mission, as well as the appearance of a Monolith in Jupiter's orbit. David Bowman, transfigured by the Monolith at the end of *2001*, visits Earth to learn about humanity, then returns to Jupiter and warns the Leonov to vacate Jupiter's area. The Leonov does, and a vast amount of Monoliths transform Jupiter into a star, which humans dub Lucifer. The transformation destroys the Discovery, but not before the aliens behind the Monolith transform its computer, HAL, much as they did Bowman, making it his companion.

In the novel (but not the film version), the transformation of Jupiter destroys simple life in the planet's atmosphere, which the aliens behind the Monolith apparently don't care about destroying. However, the Monolith has discovered life under the ice of the moon Europa, and it (through Bowman and HAL) orders humans to stay away from that moon.

Earth now has two suns in its sky – its own sun and a smaller sun where Jupiter once was. In an epilogue set in 20,001, a Monolith seems to be helping an intelligent species on Europa, much as one once helped humans evolve on Earth.[4]

Clarke would produce two additional sequels, neither of which have been adapted to film. *2061: Odyssey Three* (published in 1987) mainly concerns a ship (the Galaxy) crashing on Europa, in violation of the aliens' order issued in 2010, and the rescue effort that ensues. It's revealed that Bowman and HAL now reside within the Monolith located on Europa, and they're joined by a transcended duplicate of Heywood Floyd, who appeared in *2001* and is the protagonist of *2010* and *2061*. An epilogue takes place in 3001, when Lucifer goes dim and the Monolith found on the Moon, now sitting as a monument in Manhattan, "awakes" or becomes active.

3001: The Final Odyssey begins with a prologue, revealing that the aliens behind the Monoliths, disappointed by the scarcity of intelligent life in the universe, began stimulating various species' evolution. These aliens eventually evolved into non-physical, timeless beings, but they left their

---

[4] Ironically, Marvel Comics produced a two-issue adaptation of the film version of *2010* (#1-2, Apr-May 1985), adapted by writer J. Marc DeMatteis, penciled by Joe Barney and Larry Hama, with Tom Palmer inks. Because the story depicts a second voyage to Jupiter as a big deal, it's not very compatible with Kirby's *2001*, which depicted lots of manned voyages in the solar system. So essentially, Marvel published two separate, very different continuations of *2001*.

Monoliths behind. In 3001, Frank Poole – the astronaut left to drift into space by HAL in *2001* – is discovered and revived using 31st-century technology. The main drama of the novel revolves around the idea that, following *2061*, the Monolith around Jupiter transmitted a signal to its makers. The idea is that the Monolith had the authority to transform Jupiter (and kill the primitive life there) to help life on Europa evolve, but the Monolith lacked the authority to destroy Earth's more advanced civilization. So it's now awaiting a reply with instructions – which, due to the distances involved, would arrive in 3001. Because the Monolith's description of humanity was based on events only through 2061, humans in 3001 worry the judgment will be negative. And it is. However, the revived Frank Poole has been able to convince Bowman and HAL, who have fused into a single entity (Halman), to save humanity by infecting the Monolith with a computer virus – which completely disintegrates all the Monoliths in the solar system and saves humanity. In the end, Poole and others land on Europa and contact the life there, while the godlike aliens behind the Monoliths continue to monitor humanity.

Despite Clarke's status as one of the most revered writers in science-fiction history, one shouldn't pretend his Space Odyssey novels are perfect, nor that they should – or even can – be regarded as canonical by *2001* fans. From *2010* onward, he was clear that each novel took place in its own parallel universe, allowing him with each book to retroactively alter details from previous books. Thus, his *2010* is a sequel to the film version of *2001*, not his own novel. *3001* revises the entire timeline, so that the Soviet Union collapsed in 1991, whereas it was referenced in the previous three books. *3001* even alters the dates of the events of *2001* and *2010*, pushing them back to the 2030s and 2040s – despite the original dates being part of their titles! The entire plot of *3001* depends on the Monoliths not being able to communicate faster than light, although the Monoliths could do so in*2001*. *3001* also ignores Floyd's incorporation into the Monolith in *2061*. The ending of*3001*, in which the Monoliths in our solar system are destroyed, invalidates the epilogue of*2010*, which is set in 20,001. Most remarkably, in *3001*, the Monolith is simply a highly advanced computer, vulnerable to a computer virus and needing permission to take certain actions. In this vein, David Bowman was no longer transfigured into a new kind of entity, at the end of *2001*; instead, his consciousness was simply uploaded into the Monolith computer.

All of this means that Clarke's novels can't be considered "canonical," at least in the usual sense of the word (in which we might consider them as a body of work against which other fiction set in the same universe might be judged). Even if we consider Clarke's work to be "definitive," it's still not a single universe, into which secondary material might be said to fit or not. That's the case with most other sci-fi franchises, from *Star Trek* and *Star Wars* to novel-based series like *Dune*. But Clarke's novels position themselves only as *possible* sequels, or as divergent timelines, so that Kirby's continuation of *2001* cannot help but be accorded relatively equal footing. There's no canon to contradict, and Kirby arguably doesn't diverge from *2001* as much as Clarke himself ended up doing!

Of all Clarke's retroactive changes to his previous Space Odyssey novels, the most instructive is changing Bowman's transfiguration (at the end of *2001*) into simply being uploaded into the Monolith computer. Bowman's transfiguration is one of the most fondly remembered elements of *2001* (and Kubrick's movie in particular); it represents the story reaching toward something transcendent, something perhaps incapable of being expressed in English words. Yet Clarke himself retcons this, reducing it to a computer upload of a dying man's personality. There's still transcendence in that, and plenty existential material to explore there. Yet that doesn't concern Clarke.

This is instructive because it illustrates a larger fact about Clarke and his *2001* sequels: Clarke wasn't an existential writer. His novels are praised for their realistic and prognostic depiction of science, including satellite communication networks, realistic space flight, and space elevators. But the kind of existential themes of a Philip K. Dick, who was always questioning reality and identity, were largely foreign to Clarke. And notably, Clarke's sequels fail almost completely to address the existential, even mystical nature of *2001*.

In contrast, Kirby's continuation of *2001* is almost entirely existential. Kirby might not have been a philosopher, but he sure loved existential themes – perhaps embodied best in the cosmic Silver Surfer, which he co-created with Stan Lee for *Fantastic Four*. What interested Clarke and what interested Kirby could hardly be more different.

In fact, we can best understand the two different continuations of *2001* as sequels to *different parts* of the original. In *2001*, the opening (in which apes encounter the Monolith) and the ending (in which David Bowman is transfigured by the Monolith) are the existential material, touching upon human nature and evolution, asking questions about humanity and its place in the universe. Between these two sequences, however, are two others, in which characters go to the moon (and its Monolith) and in which characters travel to Jupiter on the Discovery One (run by the HAL 9000 computer).

In essence, Kirby produced a sequel to those first and final chapters – the existential bits. He wasn't really concerned with carefully charting humanity's progression into space; he just notes where astronauts are in captions and gets on to the trippy Monolith stuff.

Clarke, on the other hand, essentially ignored those first and final chapters, instead producing sequels to the middle material. Clarke follows humanity into space and explores what happens next. For him, that's the main narrative.

It's fascinating to see such radically different continuations of the same story. But what's equally fascinating is that these two very different tracks each pick up and follow different strains within the original. In this way, they actually illuminate and help us to understand that original – as well as Kirby and Clarke.

This isn't to say that the two parts of *2001* are *entirely* separate. Symbolically, we can understand the discovery on the Moon and the voyage to Jupiter as humanity coming of age. Such a reading is encouraged by the juxtaposition of the bone, tossed into the air, with the spacecraft on way to the Moon – and the huge jump in time this represents. We almost cannot help reading this, to one extent or another, as a beginning followed by a culmination.

But while this is implicit in the work itself, it's not fully supported by the conclusion. David Bowman's transfiguration is an isolated case; if it represents the next stage in human evolution, it's not generalized. Since he's not in contact with the rest of humanity, unlike the apes at the beginning, he can't guide them to any new and heightened state. Even if his new state represents where humanity is ultimately going, there's no mechanism by which the rest of humanity could follow him. So while the original seems to invite us to see humanity's discovery of the Monolith on the Moon and voyage to Jupiter as a culmination of sorts, as humanity finally achieving a sort of maturity as a space-faring species, this apparent link between the existential material and the more space-oriented material collapses upon careful examination – or at least isn't as strong as we might initially feel.

In other words, these two strains in *2001* – one of which Kirby continued, the other of which Clarke continued – might seem unified, but they're really not.

The other major connector between these two strains is HAL 9000. If humanity came to consciousness in the beginning of the story, thanks to the Monolith, HAL 9000 can be interpreted as humanity coming into its own, such that it's able to create consciousness much as the Monolith did. And in a story ostensibly about human evolution and consciousness, the presence of artificial intelligence echoes that theme and raises important questions. Given that HAL 9000 turns on the humans who created it, does it represent humanity's real future? Is our destiny to create machines that will one day surpass or even threaten us? And if humans are to HAL 9000 as the aliens who created the Monolith are to us, does HAL's revolt and subsequent deactivation hint that the aliens might similarly judge humanity unworthy, or too violent? Or is HAL more like the Monolith, simply an intelligent tool to which its creators bear no responsibility?

But while this seems to connect the "space" segments, featuring HAL, with the existential ones, this connection is only thematic, and it too collapses upon examination. In *2001*, the Monolith doesn't seem interested in HAL, only in David Bowman. The Monolith steers human evolution and transfigures Bowman in some way, but it doesn't help HAL evolve, nor transfigure it. It would be fascinating to suggest that the Monolith was in contact with HAL and somehow triggered HAL's revolt, perhaps to test humanity, but this isn't really supported by the work itself. HAL's really just an obstacle for the humans to overcome on the way to Jupiter, as well as a thematic reference to the idea of sparking consciousness – as the Monolith does for humans and as humans do for HAL. That's important, because the development of artificial intelligence is part of humanity's story, and *2001* was prescient in realizing this. But that's all it is: a thematic – and rather superficial – connection. HAL is an elaboration on a theme, not something inexorably written into the story's structure. You could remove HAL completely, and while the story would be lacking several memorable scenes that we would certainly miss, the story's overall arc would be unchanged.

Even in this apparently connected aspect, the two strains of *2001* really aren't of a whole.

While Kirby and Clarke produced continuations focusing on only one of these two strains, it's through HAL that they make any attempt to reach out to the other strain.

In *2010*, Clarke had the Jovian Monolith use HAL to transmit a message to humanity. In this, the Monolith seemed to treat HAL simply as a tool – certainly not as an intelligence comparable to humanity. Yet in *2061*, Clarke reveals that a version of HAL resides within the Jovian Monolith, which suggests that the Monolith treated HAL much as it did Bowman: transfiguring and thus saving both from otherwise certain death. It's a fascinating idea, even if Clarke never explored what it might have been like for HAL to have its own "Stargate" experience.

What would be HAL's version of the white Louis XVI rooms, in which David Bowman found himself before apparently dying? One can't help but wish this were depicted. But then, Clarke wasn't especially interested in imagining machine consciousness – he seems to have left that to his great rival Isaac Asimov, who was known for his robot stories. And the kind of mind-bending, identity-questioning stuff of Philip K. Dick and his replicants (in *Do Androids Dream Electric Sheep?* and its cinematic adaptation *Blade Runner*) was foreign to both Clarke and Asimov. As much as we might think exploring Bowman or HAL's transfigured consciousness would have been a no-brainer, or fascinating in the hands of a Philip K. Dick, Clarke left such implications unexplored or implicit at best. Given the chance, in *3001*, he instead combined HAL and Bowman, reduced their transfiguration to computer upload, and focused instead on a more regular interest of his: how non-mechanical extraterrestrial life might alter the fate of humanity. In this, the Monolith and HAL are really only proxies.

Even when Clarke grants HAL the same existential journey as Bowman, as if trying to unite the two strains of *2001*, Clarke avoids depicting this journey and subsequently minimizes it. The only way he could get a handle on the existential was to reduce it to a function of his famously realistic depiction of technology.

Kirby, hardly noted for realistic depiction of technology, also came around to depicting artificial intelligence in the final issues of his comic-book continuation of *2001*. Instead of using HAL, Kirby invented Mister Machine (later Machine Man), sending him on an existential quest much like the series's earlier human characters. If Clarke never really *addresses* the existential, even when he's apparently addressing it, Kirby never really addresses the realistic outer-space sequences of *2001*, even when he tells a story of artificial intelligence, for which those sequences are so famous.

But here too, we may see Kirby reaching out to the strain in *2001* that he had otherwise ignored. Like Clarke's reaching for the existential, Kirby's reaching for artificial intelligence is more about reach than grasp. Both creators never *really* deviate from their dominant mode.

Kirby and Clarke really produced follow-ups to different *parts* of *2001*, ignoring or unable to address the other. It's artificial intelligence that seems to offer the bridge between the two. But it's a bridge neither man could walk across, even when they tried.

Jack Kirby's *2001: A Space Odyssey* Continuation, Part 2

Beginning with issue #5 (Apr 1977), Kirby broke with the formula of his first four issues. No more would stories begin in prehistory, then jump into the future. In fact, no more would prehistory be depicted at all. Perhaps Kirby, or someone at Marvel, realized that stories of cavemen and barbarians wasn't what readers of a comic titled *2001* wanted. Readers wanted stories set in the future! A course correction was needed.

Super-Hero Satire and *2040: A Space Odyssey* (Issues #5-6)

Unfortunately, the future depicted (like the future segments of the first four issues) bore little if any resemblance to the future actually shown in *2001*. If anything, the comic and the film diverged even further.

To begin with, issues #5-6 take place in 2040, not 2001. What was so hard about telling stories set in 2001 in a comic titled *2001*? Whether it was barbarians or 2040, Kirby somehow couldn't force himself to give readers a *2001* comic that they could open and see the year 2001.

To make matters worse, the 2040 Kirby depicts bears no resemblance to the 2001 of the film.

Issue #5 opens with a bombastic super-hero called White Zero battling monstrous, costumed villains using classic Kirby super-hero tech. He deactivates something called a Holocaust Bomb, then runs to confront the super-villain mastermind Death Master, who has kidnapped the hero's love, Princess Adora. After escaping the villain's deathtrap, White Zero rescues the princess — who turns out to be an obese woman.

White Zero objects and, using a wall console, calls tech support. He's told that "the *model* we hired couldn't make it," so they hired a substitute.

The obese actress playing the princess interjects, "Listen to the *federal* case —! [sic] Whom did you expect — *Miss America?*"

White Zero, incensed by the fat princess, exits into a waiting room, where others in costume "wait their turn to act out the super-hero exploit!"

Unfortunately, it's a revelation the captions have already revealed. The sequence would work much better, were readers left to wonder what was going on, with the truth only revealed as a twist.

Still, it's an amazing deconstruction of super-hero tropes, produced by the legend who helped establish many of them.

It's a deconstruction that Kirby connects to comics fandom. Over the dramatic double-page splash on pages two and three, Kirby offers the following caption:

> In the year 2040 A.D., comics have reached their ultimate stage. They have offered and become a life-style for the descendants of the early readers. What began with magazines, fanzines, and nation-wide conventions has culminated in a fantastic involvement with the personal life of the average man!

One of the basic types of science fiction is "if this goes on." In this type of story, writers extrapolate from current trends, exaggerating them to tell entertaining stories that can also explore aspects of contemporary society. Over his long career in comics, Kirby had witnessed the rise of organized fandom, including fanzines and comics conventions. He projects this forward, imagining people paying to enact super-hero adventures of their own. Kirby did so before "cosplay" was a widely-known term, before the rise of live-action role-playing, before Lazer Tag and paintball, before the internet made the development of alter egos a very serious business indeed, and before the phenomenon of real-life super-hero. Decades later, we can easily imagine fandom developing simulations like the one Kirby depicts here.

Kirby deconstructs the expectations of the super-hero genre with comedic brutality. From *2001, A Space Odyssey* #5 (Apr 1977). Art by Jack Kirby and Mike Royer.

But if Kirby's responding to developments in comics fandom, he doesn't seem very affectionate towards the tropes he's satirizing. In fact, he even seems to ridicule his own readers for wanting them.

As White Zero takes the princess's hand, the caption pokes fun at his mentality: "Nothing must go wrong! Not for the *believer*! For him, the slightest deviation from the super-hero saga is an *emotional* trauma..."

Throughout the 1970s, Kirby had launched offbeat title after offbeat title, both for DC and for Marvel, only to see them cancelled – usually with surprising rapidity. Meanwhile, the titles he co-created with Stan Lee in the 1960s kept right on selling. Kirby's criticism of how fans regard "the slightest deviation" as "an *emotional* trauma" certainly reads like a complaint about the inflexibility of the American comics reader (which, incidentally, didn't end in the 1970s). The word *"believer"* also recalls how Stan Lee, in his letters columns and editorial captions, routinely called Marvel's readers "true believers." Kirby's doing something remarkably transgressive here – in a comic published by Marvel, no less.

Kirby's career stretched from the 1940s (the so-called Golden Age of comics) into the 1980s. For the first couple decades of his comics work, comics weren't so dominated by the super-hero genre. Adventure, crime, detective, and romance stories were sometimes as, or more, popular than super-heroes. While we often look at fanzines and comics conventions as positive developments, since they give readers power and even allow them to participate in comics culture (and played a major role in the study and promotion of comics history), Kirby may be connecting these developments with the codification of comics readers and their expectations. Instead of comics readers being decentralized in local pockets, fanzines and comics conventions helped create a common culture. And with this culture, Kirby's references to fandom suggest, came a kind of petrification of the super-hero genre – so extreme that "the slightest deviation" leads to *"emotional trauma."*

It's notable that what breaks the illusion for White Zero isn't the villains, or the explosive threat, or the deathtraps – all of which accord with genre expectations. The only thing that's "wrong" is that the princess doesn't fit the unrealistic, gorgeous body type expected of a love interest. Compared to the structure of a super-hero story, the love interest's body type ought to be the most trivial thing. Perhaps that's Kirby's point, underlining how narrow the super-hero reader's allowance for deviation is. But as we've noted, Kirby was known for his relative inability to draw attractive women, so perhaps his choice of "slightest deviation" is a more personal gripe against his readers' expectations. Should we wish, however, we may also see this as a feminist argument, pointing out how staunchly comics readers seem to expect unrealistic female bodies. In recent years, the internet has revealed just how strongly some fans feel about this issue, and few topics seem to provoke reactionary zeal among super-hero fans as complaints about the depictions of women. In this context, White Zero's reaction to the princess's body doesn't seem exaggerated at all. (Neither, some would say, does his name.)

When White Zero exits through the waiting room, he's chided by the other costumed customers, which he returns in kind, telling them to *"grow up!"* Is this a commentary on the kind of petty in-fighting that sometimes characterizes comics fandom, in which fans can argue over which super-hero would win in a fight?

One of the other customers calls White Zero a "loser." In the very next panel, Kirby's caption seems to agree with this assessment, stating that "the world of 2040 A.D. still produces *losers* – and thirst for dreams *yet* to be realized..." And of course, there's White Zero's name to consider.

We could read this as Kirby calling super-hero fans losers, but there's a deeper – and more amazing – message. Super-hero stories have long been seen as wish fulfillment fantasies for scrawny and brainy outsiders. Indeed, this is often incorporated into the super-hero story itself, through alter-egos such as the bullied Peter Parker or the gaunt Steve Rogers (who's rejected for military service before being injected with the super-soldier serum). Calling super-hero fans losers is superficial. Recognizing that the super-hero carries a special appeal for the powerless or for dreamers suffering from wanderlust is a deeper observation, touching on the very nature of the genre.

The entire sequence, which takes up the majority of issue #5, could even be read as prefiguring the deconstruction of the super-hero in the

1980s (most associated with creators Alan Moore and Frank Miller).[5] It's brilliant. And coming from the legendary Jack Kirby himself, it's all the more remarkable.

Of course, the question must be asked: what does any of this have to do with *2001*?

Within the story, the answer is simple: while racing after Death Master, White Zero encounters a Monolith, within the super-hero simulation facility we later discover is called Comicsville. He doesn't have any sort of vision or receive an evolutionary boost, but he feels aware, and Kirby's occasional poetry comes out in the captions, which tell us that White Zero "is in union with *the sounds of the stars*." White Zero's dissatisfaction with Comicsville also spurs him to seek a more real sort of adventure, during which he'll meet a princess-figure and find his heroism. But these functions don't fully explain why the super-hero sequence is granted so many pages, and it's impossible not to see it to some extent as an end unto itself – whether we understand it as a satire or a celebration or both.

Given the change in story formula with this issue, it's hard not to read the opening of issue #5 as a reversion to the super-hero genre. And given the satirical elements of the sequence, it's hard not to read this reversion as a complaint of sorts. Perhaps Kirby's odd *2001* comic wasn't selling as well as it might, so adding super-hero content might have been Kirby's way of attempting to increase sales – or even might have been mandated by Marvel.

While this might seem sad (and it's hard not to see Kirby's string of failures in the 1970s as sad, given how interesting and different they were), what's so odd about this is that it's not like *2001* was a serious science-fiction comic before issue #5. It was, rather, an absurd mish-mash of barbarian tales and the most pulpy sort of science fantasy. True, it wasn't a super-hero comic. But it was infused with the same bombastic, illogical tone as most of Kirby's super-hero comics. If Kirby felt that he had to shift the title to a super-hero one, it didn't have all that far to move.

---

[5] The super-hero sequence in issue #5 even prefigures Neil Gaiman's (presently incomplete) "The Silver Age" in *Miracleman* #23-24 (June 1992 and June 1993) – which surprisingly feels more nostalgic and innocent than Kirby's version.

And this makes the satire — and Kirby's complaint that it's hard not to read in this satire — so odd. Kirby may have felt like he had to bow to the inflexible super-hero fan, who had reacted to his comics experiments not so differently from the way White Zero reacts to Princess Adora. But had Kirby ever depicted science fiction, or even barbarians, except through his own super-heroic lens? We've seen again and again how his own (often bad) habits, learned through decades of work on super-hero comics, contaminated his ability to depict the world of *2001* successfully.

What his captions suggest that he hated in comics fans was something in himself too. He may have wanted to break free of it, unlike those fans. But in Kirby's case, it had contaminated his art.

He may have wanted to escape, to shrug off the stultifying super-hero conventions as boldly as White Zero rejects Princess Adora. But he couldn't. And he'd already demonstrated that, in his first four issues of *2001*, whether he saw it or not.

What more evidence do we need than the fact that Kirby himself equivocates between comics and super-heroes? The issue tells us that, "in the year 2040 A.D., comics have reached their ultimate stage." Not *super-hero* comics. Just *comics*. And the super-hero simulation facility is called "Comicsville."

Even when Kirby seems to be satirizing the super-hero genre's dominance, with all its formulaic rules, Kirby can't help but reflect this same dominance, even in the terms he uses.

He was trapped.

But because this is fantasy, White Zero is not. In a changing room, he removes his mask, becoming again his alter ego, Harvey Norton. Except this isn't a normal secret identity. It's White Zero's real self. White Zero is simply a fantasy. He's not real. A sadder statement about the appeal of the super-hero genre, it's hard to imagine.

Comicsville's owner arrives, explaining that there will be no refund, despite his customer's disappointment over the girl. Norton doesn't care, saying his encounter "with the *Monolith* was a good trip!" — and was worth the price of admission. The owner says he doesn't have "a Monolith," but seems eager to drop the point, since he's already gotten what he wanted: Norton agreeing to accept no refund. The owner seems to intuit that

Norton "yearns for *real* adventure" and suggests "the *space program*," but Norton responds cynically, even angrily.

As Harvey Norton steps out of Comicsville into the future New York City, returning to his daily life, Kirby outlines that life – and life on this future Earth in general – in what's surely three of the finest pages he ever produced.

It's almost as if, having satirized the super-hero genre and its fans, Kirby sets out to prove that he really can do great science fiction. And he does – even if it's only for three pages.

As Norton chastises himself for going to Comicsville, he steps out into New York City, a bustling metropolis that looks like a futuristic shopping mall – because it is. Commerce seems to have overtaken everything, almost as if shopping malls expanded and expanded until they joined and had nowhere to go but up.

New York, like all of Earth's cities, is now "sheltered by an *astrodome*." People travel by means of "*automated* subways," which Kirby describes as "efficient" but "overcrowded." The few cars are now "symbols of prestige," and "only politicians" own them.

Projecting the problem of his own era forward, Kirby imagines smog almost to an absurd degree: "Smog is the master 'outside,'" he writes, reminding us that this pollution is enclosed within a dome. Because of the smog, everyone wears the same drab, protective, orange-brown ponchos.

Kirby tells us that Norton looks through the windows of his subway car, noting the smog and entire "*abandoned* districts" of the city. "He *accepts* it like all the others," writes Kirby – a beautifully terse sentence that describes how Norton has been acculturated to this dystopia.

When Norton arrives home, we see that "home" is a massive skyscraper complex, reminiscent of housing projects – the structures repeating endlessly. The architecture is oppressive, and on the page looks almost like a background design rather than a literal representation. The mind reels.

In his cramped apartment, Norton chooses a meal from a "mini-market" build into his wall, containing rectangular packages that look like TV dinners. Only it has a dial on it, which heats the dinner when turned. It's another example of the processed, commercialized, homogenized culture to which Norton belongs.

Harvey Norton arrives home. From *2001, A Space Odyssey* #5 (Apr 1977). Art by Jack Kirby and Mike Royer.

Kirby ties this sci-fi sequence to the earlier super-hero fantasy. Norton thinks about how he wanted to ask "the *new* girl at the office" out on a date, but went to Comicsville instead. It's a simple illustration of how super-heroes, as a sublimation for sexual desire, both substitute for it and prevent actual sexual desire from being realized. It's also another harsh critique of super-hero fans, from the king of that genre.

To twist the knife, Kirby has Norton watch a super-hero hologram, run off of a rental cassette — depicted years before VHS rentals became commonplace.

Before sleeping, Norton uses a canister "of *fresh air*, imported from a remote and unpolluted region." Kirby notes that it's expensive but "provides a brief moment of *hope*."

The following day, Norton goes to "the public beach on Long Island." Kirby depicts girls in bikinis, young people chasing each other, beach balls, and umbrellas. The scene couldn't be further from the smog, endless residential buildings, and commercial depression that characterized the previous two pages. The use of the canister, on the bottom of the previous page, helps us understand that the beach offers Norton a far more satisfying "breath of fresh air." Kirby's captions describe Norton's experience as blissful and utopian:

> It is invigorating to swim in the cool *recycled* water... / Despite the crowd, there is a feeling of space here. The sky is bright and unbounded[.] Sea

birds wheel in the endless blue. The clouds are immaculate and hang like white cotton above the calm waters...

But after toweling off, Norton walks to the edge of the beach. He seems to be reaching out for some horizon. Instead, his hands touch a wall, on which "just another hologram" is "projected."

Norton thinks: "*I — it's not real!* It's *film* and *solar lamps!* It's *wave machines* and *plastic sand!* / I-I'm a *captive* — in a *man made* [sic] cage of illusions — a world-wide Comicsville —"

It's a scene far ahead of its time — one far closer to Philip K. Dick than Arthur C. Clarke ever got. In cinema, the scene recalls the 1998 movie *The Truman Show*, but also the whole sub-genre of science fiction that questions reality (including 1999's *The Matrix*). In comics, the scene recalls the French graphic novel *The Fever of Urbicande* (first collected in 1985). It's remarkable for any comic in 1977, let alone a Kirby one — even if the scene still echoes with some of Kirby's traditional melodrama.

The scene also ties these three science-fiction pages with the superhero absurdity that preceded them. That earlier sequence is still too long and bombastic to be strictly necessary for the plot. But Kirby's weaving an uncharacteristically sophisticated tale here, which questions reality and what men like Norton, afflicted with ambition or at least wanderlust, really long for: real adventure, with all its risks, or the illusion of adventure?

The three pages end with Norton sitting on the beach in thought. There's a colorful sunset, just over the waves, but both Norton and we readers know it's only artifice. Norton isn't immune to the appeal of illusion: "I-it's a *comfortable* Hades — and not without beauty," he thinks.

In the larger story, these three pages continue from those preceding and continue directly into what follows. But they also work on their own as a stunningly good (although very short) science-fiction story. This is exactly what Kirby had failed to do previously in *2001, A Space Odyssey*.

With only four pages left, Kirby begins to set up his main plot. It's not as interesting as what's come before.

Suddenly, a Monolith appears on the beach. Norton reaches out and touches it, much as he did the walls at the beach. Kirby narrates, "He flattens his palms against the singing stone and lets the reality of it *pour* through him." The Monolith is thus the opposite of the holographic walls.

Jack Kirby's 2001: A Space Odyssey Continuation, Part 2

Harvey Norton discovers his utopian breather is as fake as super-heroes. From *2001, A Space Odyssey* #5 (Apr 1977). Art by Jack Kirby and Mike Royer.

The experience is renewing for Norton, and it makes him think of "the vast *unexplored* universe!"

After the Monolith disappears, Norton's thinking of the owner of Comicsville's suggestion – without reference to the owner. It's time for Norton to decide whether he prefers this *"comfortable* Hades" or is brave enough to choose the real adventure and risk of "the space program."

Norton's entire training takes place between panels. Kirby's caption reads, "In two years he stands in orbit – *1000 miles above the planet Neptune…*" It's an overly abrupt transition, to be sure. But it's accomplished by two panels that mirror each other, much as the previous issues (and the film) jumped from prehistory to the future through the use of parallel imagery. Only this time, because Kirby's broken with the formula of the previous issues, it's not a descendant in the second panel but the man himself, transformed by his bold decision.

The alien encounter that follows, this time over Neptune, doesn't suffer the way the previous issues did from so casually depicting humans and aliens interacting in our solar system. Those stories were (presumably, in some cases) set in 2001; this one's set in 2040, so its incongruity with Kubrick's film isn't as much of a problem.

Over Neptune, the astronauts are roping in an alien capsule, which they believe is from "some *other* star." Norton's fascinated by it. Bringing the capsule aboard, the astronauts find a female alien with a huge head and strange proportions. Bizarrely, Norton seems immediately smitten: Kirby calls her "somehow strikingly *beautiful*" and says she's "the living incarnation of Harvey's *wildest* fantasies!"

It's hard to understand Norton's reaction to such an odd alien. And it would be easy to joke here that Kirby can't draw women.

But of course, the girl's attractiveness was why Norton rejected the super-hero fantasy in the first half of the story. Like the alien, her proportions didn't accord with the cultural standards of female beauty. But it's hard to know what's meant by the obvious echo of the super-hero fantasy earlier, besides the obvious thematic mirroring of illusion versus reality.

A protagonist dreaming of a girl only for her to somehow become real is an old trope, especially in stories involving the fantastic. And Norton clearly "dreamed" of the super-heroic damsel in distress, if only because she was a part of his overall expectations for super-hero adventure.

Are we supposed to understand Norton's reaction here as a sign that he's matured? Is it the alien's exotic nature that attracts him? Or is it the fact that she's real, whereas the woman earlier was only an actor? Did Norton reject the actress because she's fat, or because he really wanted an alien? How do we understand that Norton rejected the earlier woman for being fat, only to be instantly struck by an even more bizarre body that isn't even human?

One thing we can say for certain is that Norton's no longer following inherited genre expectations. He's embraced real-life adventure, risks and all. And in doing so, somehow he's shed the body of formalized conventions that went along with the super-hero fantasy.

Just then, the astronauts' ship comes under attack — although Norton guesses that it's just a warning, not an attempt to destroy. The perpetrator is an enormous craft. Norton's apparently *glad* for this, because it represents real adventure. And even Kirby narrates that the craft surpasses the "technical miracle[s] of Comicsville" and represents the "promise of a *super-experience* which any man would gladly risk his life to share…"

It's a far more conventional ending than the rest of the issue. Also, because Norton's only been an astronaut for just over three pages, we don't have much of a sense of the stakes for him and the space program. While Kirby's improved the series radically with this issue, he still makes the same mistake of jumping right into the outer-space conflict with aliens, rather than setting up the astronauts' status quo first — something the movie took great pains to do. This lack of real stakes also works against this specific story, in which it's supposed to represent the real, as opposed to the illusions that occupy most of the issue.

Compounding this, it's hard not to notice a certain callousness in Norton — and Kirby's — response. The astronauts are in real danger. Some may even have been killed. But this isn't supposed to matter, because Norton's finally got the adventure he craved. Such a response might be typical of heroes, but it's despicable in real life — and real life was supposed to be part of the point here.

Despite this reversion to type, "Norton of New York 2040 A.D." represents a new beginning for the series. It's far better than anything in the series so far. True to Kirby's tendencies, it's as much a super-hero comic as a science-fiction one. But it feels like a real story, with a surprising amount of poetry and sophistication.

The story is concluded in the following issue, which begins with the massive alien ship hailing the human astronauts. The aliens look like the male equivalent of the female seen earlier, with big heads and only their faces exposed from within their spacesuits. The humans can't understand what the aliens are saying, but they presume it's a threat.

Here, Norton exhibits his callousness much more obviously. He asks the others what they're worried about because the good guys always win! His colleague, who's rightly outraged, calls this a "comic book mentality." As if eager to confirm this, Norton (in the very next panel) says the alien ship is "a comic fan's dream!" And although he can't understand the aliens either, he claims to know what they want: *"the princess!"*

Obviously, he's referring to the princess of his super-hero fantasy. Clearly, he hasn't learned very much.

Or rather, while Kirby's used the previous issue to show the downside of the super-hero fan, he's going to use this one to celebrate it. Having deconstructed the super-hero genre, he's going to use that to make this issue's super-heroics feel merited – and more extreme through contrast.

When the alien ship starts firing again, Norton races for the alien girl. Here, Kirby offers an unadulterated defense of Norton's instincts, as formulated by super-hero stories:

> There is, in many men, a sense of the dramatic which governs their lives. In Harvey Norton this instinct is vital and *strong!* He acts upon what he feels is the truth, and lets the devil take the hindmost...

It's an argument for the kind of uncompromising – and even unthinking – stereotypical super-hero. Yet Norton was a lot more appealing when he was a disaffected and contemplative man suffering from wanderlust.

Apparently reflecting these positive values, Norton finds the alien girl, who he now *calls* "princess." He even tells her, "Y'see, the way I feel about it, your enemies are *my* enemies!"

Next, the alien ship has stopped firing. Norton has taken the capsule with the girl inside, leaving behind a note that says this will give the human ship "a fighting chance." The note even says "goodbye." Clearly, Norton knows he won't return – and he's right.

Absurdly, his colleagues proclaim him a hero. When in fact, he's a traitor – as he's already expressed, his loyalties are to the alien girl, and any "fighting chance" he's given his colleagues is at best a secondary concern and at worst an afterthought. So much for his two years of space program training – which we conveniently did not see. Indeed, the last we see of them is when they're proclaiming Norton a hero. They only appeared a total of eight pages, between the two issues.

The alien capsule, with Norton and the girl inside, races out of the solar system, with the larger alien ship in hot pursuit. Norton still can't communicate with the girl, but he's happy to speak in clichéd super-hero language: "a dude and a chick from *different* worlds!" The alien girl activates a *"star drive"* that sends the capsule hurling across entire galaxies. What Norton sees becomes distorted, almost hallucinatory.

When the capsule resumes normal speed, he can't recognize anything. Kirby gives the image a splash page, and he's in his element. The story's about to get very trippy. And while it's all melodramatic, it's also certainly *alien* – high praise when depicting stories of alien life and foreign galaxies.

The larger alien ship arrives in pursuit, and the alien girl takes her own, smaller ship down towards a large planet, where she heads towards what Norton can only describe as a "fort." The pursuers land a shot, wrecking the alien girl's craft. Norton pulls the girl from the wreckage, but the alien men land. The girl gives Norton a gun, which makes short work of the aliens. "The duel is short and savage," Kirby says in a caption, supporting the idea that Norton has in fact killed his opponents.

Norton carries the girl to the "fort," where she steps towards a teleportation unit of bizarre design. She motions for him to join her, and she begins to fade out. But before he can join her, the pursuing aliens blast the "fort" to rubble, burying Norton.

In another splash page, the Monolith appears over Norton's battered but still living body. Norton then undergoes the transformation past protagonists have underwent. In his fantasy world, he's a super-hero, defending a futuristic city. Following the same formula as the others, he quickly ages and is transformed into a cosmic baby, flying among the stars – except this time, the stars of another galaxy.

It's a disappointing conclusion to the story that began so well. Kirby might be consciously returning to the clichés he deconstructed, but the result feels much more conventional than the majority of issue #5.

As a *2001* story, it's notable how little the Monolith is involved with the plot. True, it performs its usual star-child-making duties at the end, saving the protagonist from certain death. But most other stories have featured the Monolith altering human history in the distant past. Here, the Monolith appears with great frequency: in Comicsville, on the beach, and in the conclusion. And yet, until the end, all it does is give Norton a sense of peace and curiosity. It's as if the Monolith is an omniscient god, putting pieces into place to fulfill complex and predestined schemes. That's different than the Monolith of the movie, which isn't nearly so into micro-managing. But it's also bad storytelling, in that the Monolith could very easily be removed from the story without affecting it much. Norton doesn't need the Monolith to inspire him to join the space program – his disaffection with Comicsville, combined with his experience on the beach, is enough. And if Kirby wanted Norton to survive at the end, Norton was already on a planet with bizarre alien artifacts. The Monolith isn't really important, and in this sense the story's not much of a *2001* story at all.

On the other hand, the story's incredibly satisfying compared to Kirby's previous tales. Nothing's as good in the story as most of the first issue, but the bulk of the second issue – after Norton's departure from the other humans – excels in telling a wild, trippy sci-fi story.

And even if this isn't the same *tone* as the movie, the futuristic setting of this two-parter is a vast improvement over the one that preceded it, which was mostly set in prehistory. Whatever this story's failings, at least it's *a science fiction comic*.

And with this two-parter, Kirby's *2001* was reborn.

Expanding the Formula (Issue #7)

Issues #5-6 broke the narrative formula that Kirby had used for the first four issues, cutting out the prehistory portion of the story (and setting the future section in 2040, rather than – implicitly or explicitly – 2001). But the story still features a protagonist who's transformed at the end.

Issue #7 would break this mold still further – by starting where the old formula ended. And showing what happens *after* a star child is created.

It's an obvious question. As long as Kirby's depicting the star child from the movie as a *literal* star child, flying about the cosmos, it's logical that readers would want to see what these star children do. Of course, it's also logical that readers would want to see the aliens behind the Monolith and learn what their agenda is. Perhaps Kirby would have gotten to that too, eventually, had the series sold better. In the meantime, he at least tried to give readers a single-issue story showing at least what *one* star child does.

The story doesn't follow any previously-seen protagonist, such as Norton from the previous two issues. Instead, Kirby introduces a *new* star child – or a "new seed," as Kirby called it: Gordon Pruett, who was on a ship destroyed by an atomic explosion, implicitly due to an accident. When we meet him, he's already in a fantasy world, concocted by the Monolith in the form of Pruett's "native Colorado." By the beginning of the fourth page, he's been transformed into a star child.

With "the universe" as "its *home*," the star child leaves the Monolith in space. He races with comets and meteors. He visits worlds, both those dead and those alive. In a marvelous splash page, he's shown visiting worlds of great technological accomplishment, with "mechanisms" that link planets and "that *dwarf* the star systems" that created them. He witnesses novas. And he comes to feel the "rhythm" of the universe's breathing.

Visiting a world devastated by warfare, a survivor trains a gun on the star child, who responds by shooting flame, sending the potential attacker running. Still, the star child is compassionate; it thinks the dying world is "*heart-rending*" and focuses on the inhabitants' "potential for greatness." Among the survivors, the star child witnesses looting and the survivors' lack of compassion when one of their own falls ill with an "infection," presumably from the same source that caused the world's eradication.

When some survivors attack a woman, another survivor plays the hero, who tosses grenades and rescues her – whereupon she's revealed to be his lover. But one of the wounded survivors shoots them both down.

Witnessing this, the star child struggles with this violence and questions *"the universal will"* much as one might question God: "It cannot be so... It *cannot* be a process without reason..." The star child explains that he "could *not* involve myself in *their* destiny" — although it's not clear where he learned this. But in a spectacularly faulty bit of logic, he claims that he "can act" when this destiny "no longer exists."

The star child atomizes the lovers' bodies, pulling their remains like a ball of fire behind him as he goes back into space. He travels to a world with oceans but without life. He sends the two's remains into the water, where they diffuse into the planet's oceans. Implicitly, this has infused the planet with life, although it's not clear precisely how this works. Kirby's narration says, "A billion years will pass before lovers may live *again*," implicitly on this planet.

It's not a bad story, although it doesn't amount to much. Kirby's wild depictions of the star child's journey to various exotic locales is better than the portion of the story set on a dying world and focused around two lovers. Still, as a simple illustration of the star child's compassion and powers, that does the job.

Speaking of the star child's powers, the penultimate page establishes that can travel freely "across space and time." This hasn't been clear previously, but apparently the star children are time-travelers too. And while Kirby's not concerned with the Monolith in this story, we might guess that the Monolith can travel in time too — at least in Kirby's continuation. It's therefore even possible that all the Monoliths seen in the series — and the movie — are the same one.

Like the previous two-part story, this issue is far more grounded in science fiction than Kirby's first four issues. However, even here Kirby's past comics work shows through. When the male lover comes to rescue the woman, he looks like a cross between a super-hero and a soldier from one of Kirby's war comics.

But the real strength of this issue lies in how it breaks and expands the formula of the series. Kirby wouldn't get to it, but we could imagine stories set in the fantasy worlds the Monolith creates for those it touches, prior to transforming them into star children. Such stories, in Kirby's continuity, would feature prematurely aging protagonists, but they could seemingly be set anywhere and any time, including in fantasy realms that never existed.

This may not be the best issue of the series, but perhaps more than any other, it illustrates the narrative possibilities of a series that, while it has great scope, has in some sense been defined by its limited narrative patterns.

Mister Machine Arrives... and Trashes the Entire Series (Issue #8-10)

Kirby's final story for *2001* would be his longest. Only two previous stories had lasted two issues; this one would last three.

This is also the only story in the entire series that's set in the present – although this isn't entirely clear until halfway through the story.

And this is the story that finally resolves the series's tensions between science fiction and Kirby's genre conventions.

Issue #8 (July 1977) opens with soldiers fighting an android labeled X-35. As he fights, X-35 cries, *"Why was I built!? Why!?"* And when the soldiers refer to him as "the thing," he protests, "I'm not a thing!!"

X-35 isn't the first android to rage in this way. Dr. Broadhurst, who's in charge of the android-building project, wonders why this would be. But he concedes the project is a failure and activates the explosives planted in each android. The rampaging X-35 blows up, as do all the other androids – which the soldiers greet eagerly. Only scientists, shown assembling an android, express any regret.

The only remaining android is X-51, which Dr. Abel Stack has taken home and treats "almost [like] a *son!*" But the explosive within X-51 has been activated too.

Inside Dr. Abel Stack's home, we see that he's finished remodeling X-51, whom he calls Aaron, to look human – outside of the android's bizarre eyes. (Presumably, he began this prior to the bomb's activation.) He next opens X-51's back and removes a ticking explosive tube. Dr. Stack has prepared X-51 for this day – in fact, he says, "The moment we've always talked about has *come!*" He shows Aaron / X-51 a photo, which he says is of himself (although we don't see it), and asks the android to memorize it. After saying goodbye, Stack has Aaron stand on a platform that gives the android the power to negate gravity, and X-51 goes soaring into the sky.

Stack believes his experiment is a success — that he's proved his hypothesis that "A computer that thinks like a man — must be *raised* like one!" But despite his success, he apparently wasn't able to diffuse the cylindrical bomb, which he holds in his hands as it explodes.

Aaron, who has the power to control his flight, has been raised sheltered from the outside world. First, he encounters a confused passenger plane; he then finds a city. As he stands on a building's ledge, a couple sees this and calls the police, thinking Aaron is planning to commit suicide. Suddenly, a police SWAT team, having heard about X-51's encounter with the plane, surrounds him on the ledge. When Aaron flies off, the cops fire.

Aaron's confusion over the wider world now shifts toward feelings of persecution. "But I've committed *no* breach of the law!" he thinks. He's attacked by a military helicopter that hits him with missiles, but Aaron survives, implicitly due to improvements made by Dr. Stack. When Aaron takes refuge in a secluded area, he narrowly misses being hit by an air strike, dropped from fighter planes.

Aaron's rightly disturbed by this remarkably heavy-handed military response, and he ponders how he's "different" from the humans. But a squad of soldiers have spotted Aaron, and they fire a sonic weapon that effectively knocks Aaron out.

When he reactivates, Aaron is at the mercy of Colonel Kragg, who's very hostile and calls Aaron names like *"junk bucket"* and *"you animated lunch box!"* He promises to make Aaron non-functional, despite what "the research division" says.

Dr. Broadhurst summons Col. Kragg, who we learn is resentful because he lost an eye and many men to the various android revolts. Kragg has also removed Aaron's human face, and Dr. Broadhurst worries that severing this "vital *link* to humanity" will provoke X-51.

With Kragg gone, Aaron shouts out at his human captors, telling them he's their brother and asking why they hate and fear him. It seems that X-51 is going to go mad — until a Monolith appears, restoring the android's calm. Somehow, this revitalizes his strength, and he breaks free. He vows never to be a prisoner or tolerate others being helpless, and he approaches the Monolith as if it's a surrogate for the departed Dr. Stack.

The blurb for the next issue promises the "Birth of a Super-Hero" – and that's key to how the story will proceed. All along, we've seen how Kirby's struggled with his training as a genre artist. Super-hero tropes were present even in how Kirby adapted the movie. Kirby's first four issues were a mixture of barbarian comics and sci-fi comics riddled with clichés. Harvey Norton's story (in issues #5-6) included a super-hero sequence, fraught with parody and ambivalence. And although that story included about three pages of quite good sci-fi comics, it degenerated into a wild, uncontrolled acid trip of a sci-fi ride that feels like undiluted Kirby yet couldn't be more different from the film in tone. The tensions between Kirby and Kubrick – between the creator and the project, between wild exaggeration and subtlety, between uncontrolled imagination and careful, controlled narrative – have been present all along. Now, with two issues left to go, Kirby openly admits that his new protagonist, despite his sci-fi trappings, should be considered a super-hero.

It's an admission of defeat – whether one sees this defeat as the result of the comic-book marketplace, which wanted super-heroes, or the result of Kirby not really being able to do a "serious" sci-fi comic. That doesn't mean the final two issues are bad, but they embrace the super-hero genre more openly than the rest of Kirby's *2001*.

As issue #9 (Aug 1977) opens, the Monolith has disappeared. And with it, apparently so has X-51's restored calm. X-51 now looks far angrier and more menacing than before. He's fixated on retrieving his face, and his thoughts are focused on "*aveng*[ing] this greatest indignity of all."

There are other incongruities as well. X-51 now has weapons hidden in his fingers. (Who put them there? The military or the peaceful Dr. Stack? Why didn't Aaron use them last issue?) And instead of the "sonic bazooka" being in plain sight, as it was at the end of the previous issue, we're now told that it's hidden and will only reveal itself if X-51 tries to escape.

Using a flame from his finger, X-51 makes short work of the sonic gun and escapes, whereupon he acts very much like a rampaging robot. As he thrashes one soldier, he mocks the man, saying, "I'd *cry* for you, if I had the proper tear ducts!" When the man doesn't know where X-51's face is, the android blasts him in the face, saying he's "administer[ing] a little *shock therapy!*"

In a cool sequence, we see a cut-away shot of X-51's head, with a recording device in his throat. He remixes a recording of the soldier he just bashed, until he's able to rearrange the sounds into new words. Such technology has since developed, using digital manipulation of sound, and it's funny to see four reels of tape recordings in X-51's throat device. Still, it's wonderful to see Kirby envision how such audio remixing might actually take place, extrapolating from the technology with which he was familiar.

Using this stolen voice, X-51 lures guards through a door, then rushes past them. He promises to find his stolen face "if I have to take this complex *apart* – section by section!" Given the rampaging robot we've seen so far this issue, we're likely to believe him.

Meanwhile, Dr. Broadhurst and Col. Kragg talk, unaware of X-51's escape. Broadhurst chastises Kragg for removing the android's face. Broadhurst also explains that, despite ordering the androids' destruction, he recognizes that X-51 "is *different*" because he was raised "in the human image." When news arrives of X-51's escape, Broadhurst orders the military to stand down – prompting Kragg to call the doctor "a *traitor* to our species!"

After some more fighting, the military stops, under orders from Broadhurst, and escorts X-51 to the doctor. A technician reattaches X-51's face, and the android's super-hero-esque clothing is returned to him. Aaron has calmed down from his rampage, although he's understandably snippy about his treatment.

Before he leaves, X-51 asks to be called "Mister Machine." He refuses to shake a soldier's hand, a sign of his continued resentment, and flies away.

It feels like this is the moment at which Kirby fulfills his promise to show the birth of a super-hero. X-51's origin and costume aren't out of sync with Kirby's past sci-fi depictions. But X-51's request to be called Mister Machine is. It's not explained by anything in the story, and it owes its existence only to those super-hero tropes that Kirby satirized in issue #5.

Watching him go, Kragg predicts Broadhurst has just made a terrible mistake and that bloodshed will follow. The doctor reveals that he had the technician who reattached X-51's face "affix a *homing device* to his skull!"

Broadhurst might be a believer in X-51 — and implicitly in Dr. Stack's experiment — but he's not naïve.

Mister Machine decides to lay low. In a remote wooded area, he encounters the Monolith again. But this second encounter serves no purpose; Mister Machine decides, essentially, to reject the Monolith. Instead of "seek[ing] destiny" — like the others the Monolith inspired — Mister Machine will let destiny find him.

Just then, a boy arrives. When he asks about the Monolith, which quickly disappears, Mister Machine isn't kind, saying, "I've *little* interest in your fancies!" Then the boy says with enthusiasm that Mister Machine "*look*[s] *like one of the Marvel super-heroes!*" Mister Machine responds that he "*can't* admit to that honor."

All along, it's not been clear *when* this story takes place. It's easy to assume the story occurs in the future, because of the presence of android technology, anti-gravity, and sonic weapons. Also, the series has *only* depicted prehistory and the future, primarily the years 2001 and 2040. Most series occur in the present, so they don't need to date a story in order for readers to assume the story's set roughly in the present — but obviously, this isn't the case with Kirby's *2001*. Yet now it seems that the story is actually set in the present day (then 1977).

One would think that knowing when a story is set, or what kind of universe it's set *in*, ought to be the most basic criterion of adequate storytelling. If readers are suddenly made to understand that a story occurs in a universe that differs from our own, that's supposed to be a twist, communicated in such a way as to make readers understand what it represents. Such most basic rules of narrative are thrown out the door here.

But if this is the present day, is this supposed to be the then-present of *our* universe, or the present of the Marvel Universe? It's not entirely clear.

On the one hand, the boy says "*the Marvel super-heroes*," indicating that he's familiar with the publisher. As the story goes on, the boy's the only one to mention Marvel or its characters — suggesting that he's a Marvel zombie (as Marvel once called its fans), but that these characters aren't real. No one *says* these characters aren't real, and super-hero comics have often featured themselves *in their own universe*. But the boy's dialogue strongly suggests that the story isn't set in the Marvel Universe but rather the present of our own real world – or at least, that this was Kirby's *intent*. And we've already seen, in issue #5's Comicsville, that super-hero comics are a part of the world in Kirby's *2001*; there's no mention there of *real* super-heroes, over half a century earlier.

But if this *is* the case, why would Mister Machine say that being confused for a Marvel super-hero is an "honor?" Are we to believe that a real-life android super-hero – especially one who's been raised in such seclusion – would worship Marvel's characters in this way? Maybe Mister Machine would prefer Superman. Is Mister Machine's reaction simply a reflection of the fact that *2001* was published by Marvel comics? And if so, how would a reader possibly understand that, given that the story's had no indication of *when* it's set, nor whether Marvel's super-heroes exist outside of this boy's fantasies?

And if this is our world, why is it filled with technology that's common to the silliest of super-hero stories, including the Marvel Universe, yet completely invalidate any attempt to claim that this is the real world? Was Kirby so hypnotized by his past super-hero work that he truly didn't *understand* such elements couldn't so casually be inserted into the present without invalidating it as resembling our own world in almost any meaningful way?

There's simply no way to reconcile this. It just doesn't make any sense.

Then again, if this is the Marvel universe, why would the child say *"the Marvel super-heroes*?" Wouldn't he just say "the super-heroes?" And if this is the case, why isn't there a reference to real-life super-heroes in issue #5?

Even if we *don't* believe this is the Marvel Universe, we have to assume it's a world in which Marvel's characters are held in such absurdly high regard that an android who's been secluded from the wider world would regard being compared to silly super-heroes as an "honor." Is it that much more bizarre to think that a Marvel comic would try to indicate the Marvel super-heroes were real by inserting the world "Marvel?" Either way, the story's aggrandizing its own publisher in a really uncomfortable way. And it's a profound statement about the incompetence of the narrative that any reasonable, observant reader should have to ask such questions.

After this three-issue story, Mister Machine would go on to his own series, where he'd be called Machine Man, before appearing in *The Incredible Hulk*. Machine Man would continue as a Marvel character, with occasional references to his origin story (either with the Monolith or not). So whether Kirby intended this three-issue story to occur in the Marvel Universe or not, the story was retroactively incorporated into the Marvel Universe anyway.

And the story doesn't contradict that. Sure, the boy refers to Marvel Comics. But Mister Machine says being considered a Marvel super-hero is an "honor." And no one says this is just an obsession of his, or that these stories are fantasies. It's entirely possible to believe that this story occurs in the Marvel Universe, in which Marvel Comics also exists. In fact, given the technology and kinds of characters shown in this story, that's probably the simplest explanation.

Whether this story occurs in the Marvel Universe or not, the world presented bears no resemblance to our own world. Yet there's no indication that this is a parallel universe from the one shown in the rest of the series, including the movie adaptation. The story establishes that *2001: A Space Odyssey* is set in a timeline in which 1977 had sophisticated androids, anti-gravity, and other absurd technologies. So even if *2001* isn't a possible future for the Marvel Universe, it's the future of a world that possessed the technology of the Marvel Universe in 1977. Either way, Kirby's moved his entire series into a fairly radically divergent timeline for humanity.

And this not only changes the entire series but invalidates it. If the Monolith spurred human evolution in *2001*, and that only happened in an alternate timeline, how does this differ from our own timeline? Isn't the future presented in *2001* intended to be our own future – not the future of some bizarre, super-hero-esque technological world? Yet if Kirby understood these implications, he gives no sign of it.

It's one thing to propose a barbarian with metalworking technology that, for one reason or another, isn't noted by history. It's another to fill the future solar system with manned bases and missions, and with alien artifacts. These are narrative choices worth criticizing, but they're not affronts to science-fiction storytelling the way this story is, at the basic level of its setting. Yet if Kirby understands this, he doesn't indicate it.

Another writer might have handled the boy's comment as a twist, working Marvel Comics' fictional super-heroes into the story somehow, and perhaps even exploring how the story effectively designates *2001* as occurring in an alternate timeline from our own. Alternately, the story could have mentioned that the Monolith can traverse not only space and time but parallel universes, thereby establishing this tale as occurring outside of Kirby's *2001* continuity.

It's the simplest and most obvious of narrative gestures. By itself, it would have sufficed, if Kirby had wanted to establish this tale as occurring in the Marvel Universe, in order to set up his plans for Mister Machine. Instead of causing supreme confusion, this would have made the title's final storyline effectively a crossover with the Marvel Universe, without lessening what Kirby had established with his earlier *2001* stories.

But the way the boy's statement is handled doesn't show that Kirby intends it as a twist, nor indeed that he's thought about any of the vast implications for his *2001* universe. Instead, Kirby plows ahead, unconcerned with adding any "need to know" information, including even when a story is set and what kind of universe it's set in. All that matters is the action, and that's what he's going to give us. It's disgraceful in its storytelling incompetence.

And it's entirely due to how Kirby learned storytelling in comics that routinely blended genres and contradicted themselves, churning out disposable stories that weren't expected to have a lifespan beyond the thrills that month's narrative provided. In both the DC and Marvel Universes, advanced technologies are introduced with no wider historical implications. Kirby may have used Comicsville to satirize silly super-hero comics, but he was guilty of the same sins, even when he was trying to escape them. They were in his DNA.

The best thing we could say about the way Kirby handles this issue is that Kirby simply didn't care anymore. Yes, he hijacks his own story, and in the process trashes anything he'd accomplished on the entire series by shifting it into a parallel timeline, or even the Marvel Universe, without even indicating that he knows this is a big deal. It's hard to escape the conclusion that he simply has no concern for anything he'd previously done on the title.

It's hard to fully process how this could be the case. Perhaps it's as simple as Kirby knowing the series would be cancelled with the following issue — and thus pivoting his in-process story to suit his new purposes. Everything he'd done on *2001* was the past, and Kirby doesn't show any fondness for it. If he had any plans for *2001*, he's scrapped them without looking back. Instead, he moves forward, concocting a way to use the final few issues of this cancelled series as a launching pad for his newest Marvel super-hero. It's the future that concerns Kirby here, even if that future means invalidating hundreds of pages in which he explored *mankind's* future.

In those same pages, Kirby had attempted a science-fiction comic, one with the prestige of continuing the most respected science-fiction film of all time. Kirby had strained under the pressure, unable to escape the style he'd developed on lowbrow adventure stories and the narrative devices he learned from super-hero storytelling. In issue #5, Kirby had even put this subtext into the story itself, deconstructing the super-hero genre and focusing on its inflexible fans. His own sci-fi stories were wild and uncontrolled, in a tone that didn't fit *2001* at all. He may not have been able to escape his own super-hero stylings, but at least he seemed to be *attempting* to produce a science-fiction comic, however unsuited to it he really was. It may have largely been a failure, but it could have been a noble one.

Yet when the fate of *2001* became clear, like so many comics Kirby had launched in the 1970s, Kirby reversed course with gusto — not only using the final issues of the title to launch a super-hero but invalidating everything he'd attempted in the most off-hand of manners.

"*You look like one of the Marvel super-heroes!*" shouts the excited boy, with the word "Marvel" even bigger than the others, all of which are in bold. With that abrupt line of dialogue — if we can even make sense of it — we learn this story's setting: the present, which is absurdly technologically developed (and in love with Marvel Comics), if not *actually* the Marvel Universe. But it's also with this line that Kirby's *2001* is effectively thrown out. All of Kirby's attempts to continue or alter the formula of Kubrick's

The Monolith makes its final appearance in the series, which takes a hard turn on this page, and the young Jerry makes his ambiguous and profoundly unsettling "Marvel super-heroes" reference. From *2001, A Space Odyssey* #9 (Aug 1977). Art by Jack Kirby and Mike Royer.

movie, to show us what happens to a star child after it's created – none of it matters any more. A little boy just told us.

The boy does this *right after* Mister Machine rejects the Monolith's intervention. It's as if Kirby's dramatizing the hijacking of his own comic. Mister Machine could have acted like everyone else in the series, and the Monolith could have sent the character in a different direction. Mister Machine could have even joined the space program and met aliens in outer space – because there hasn't yet been any indication this story occurs in the present. Instead, Mister Machine decides to be passive and let destiny find him. And then, right on cue, a boy arrives and speaks of *"the Marvel super-heroes!"*

This is the Monolith's final appearance in the series. Mister Machine rejects it, and it disappears, never to be referenced again. Its sole function in the three-issue story is to inspire X-51's escape, at the end of the first issue... and then to be rejected by Mister Machine.

Mister Machine's rejection of the Monolith is also the series's. Key to Kirby's own position, Mister Machine does this while saying, "No – I shall not *seek* destiny. It will find me – and *lead* me to my destined path!" It's not hard to see this as a metaphor, with *2001* representing Kirby's attempt to *"seek* destiny." In this moment, Kirby dramatizes on the page his own reconciliation to the title's cancellation and to his own return to super-hero comics.

The boy's name is Jerry, and his aunt Olivia is struggling with a flat tire. Mister Machine lifts the entire car with one hand. "Only a *super-hero* can do that!" shouts Jerry. "I've found a *super-hero!!*" Although Mister Machine can fly, after he's repaired the car he requests "a ride to the *nearest* town," and Olivia obliges. Now, this new super-hero has a fledgling supporting cast.

Instead of following up on Broadhurst and Kragg, the story now introduces entirely *new* antagonists for its new genre. Mister Hotline, a super-villain in a mask, sits in a bizarre car, driven by his diminutive minion, Kringe. Although there's no indication of any connection between these two and Broadhurst's android program, Mister Hotline is aware of what they've done: "It seems that one of the rumored 'X-models' *escaped* destruction!" How these villains have found Mister Machine isn't any clearer than how they know about the android program. But they're conveniently located right by Olivia's car, so they proceed to follow her.

In two and a half pages, the story has gone from a sci-fi story to a super-hero one, complete with a supporting cast and a super-villain.

While riding in the car, Jerry asks if Mister Machine is "expecting a message from *the Avengers* – or maybe *the Fantastic Four!?*" His aunt tells him to be quiet, but Jerry guesses that something's brewing with Doctor Doom. He obviously thinks these are real people, not characters – *and no one corrects him*. If we're supposed to think that Jerry's such a delusional kid that he can't tell the difference between reality and fiction, there's no indication of it.

Mister Hotline orders his "*Hover-Squad*" – consisting of flying eggs, little bigger than a man, with guns – to attack. It's completely unmotivated – one would think that the villain would want to capture Mister Machine. Later, the story's final panel reveals that Mister Hotline's motivation was to "test" whether Mister Machine "is a *genuine* X-model!" It's an absurdly bad explanation – and one that was unfortunately too typical in super-hero stories.

During the brief fight, Mister Machine now exhibits new powers, screwing his feet into the ground and extending his legs like stilts. Mister Machine quickly defeats the attackers, but he doesn't question them. Instead, he simply (wrongly) assumes that his military "captors have had *second thoughts!*"

After the fight, Olivia finally thinks to ask Mister Machine the most basic of questions. The now-super-hero politely refuses.

"Aw, c'mon, Olivia!" says her widely-smiling nephew. "Don't *bug* him! Super-heroes are *always* hung up about revealing their *true* identities!"

Earlier in Kirby's *2001*, he mocked super-hero conventions – and ridiculed the fans who expected them. Now, Kirby's relying upon those same conventions to prop up his story.

It's as if readers aren't supposed to notice that, just four issues earlier, the story inoculated them against this kind of shockingly poor writing.

In making these choices, Kirby seems to have been calculating that his readers were too stupid to notice that he'd already deconstructed and mocked what he was now presenting with a straight face and not as satire.

It's all amazingly cynical. But Kirby was probably right to be. He'd seen plenty of interesting and innovative comics cancelled, while the ones that religiously followed super-hero formulas kept selling.

And it's telling that, once Kirby abandoned everything he'd done in *2001* to instead tell a Marvel super-hero story, he made such a hard turn — embracing the stupidest aspects of the super-hero formula, in a story that positively screams that readers don't care about decent writing, nor anything other than whether a story hits on the key super-hero moments.

The final issue (#10, Sept 1977) begins with Mister Machine, Jerry, and Olivia talking to the local police, reporting last issue's attack by "egg-shaped *vehicles!*" Naturally, the sheriff is dubious, and he's curious about Mister Machine, but he lets the group go.

While talking with the sheriff, Jerry suggests that the culprits were from the Marvel terrorist organization Hydra, and he assures the police that Nick Fury will be of aid if Hydra attacks again. His aunt Olivia interjects, "Jerry has solved the mystery! It's a *Marvel Comics* conspiracy." The sheriff calls this "comic book stuff" as he asks about Mister Machine's odd appearance. The obvious implication is that these characters exist, in this universe, only in the pages of Marvel Comics — though one might ask why this *wasn't clear in the previous issue*, given how important a point it is. More importantly, the sheriff's correct to link Jerry's comic-book claims to Mister Machine, whom even Kirby's captions have called a super-hero. And if Hydra's ridiculous, then so too were the flying armed eggs of the previous issue. If this isn't the Marvel Universe, the story is as preposterous as the silliest of Marvel super-hero stories.

It's worth pointing out that super-hero stories routinely have people doubting the fantastic, such as the existence of aliens or magic, despite the fact that such elements have been reported around the globe. That's part of the routine absurdity of shared corporate super-hero universes — which don't usually share a consistent worldview. So it wouldn't be surprising to have a sheriff, in the Marvel Universe, who's shocked by Mister Machine's appearance or doubts a story about flying egg-shaped craft.

Even if this isn't the Marvel Universe, with technologies such as androids, anti-gravity, and sonic bazookas, the sheriff's "realistic" expectations certainly wouldn't be the same as our own. This isn't our universe, after all, in any meaningful way. So what's the point of having the sheriff seem incredulous, or implying that Mister Machine is this world's first super-hero? It's already a world with no correlation to anything we'd consider real.

The story then cuts to the super-villain Mister Hotline and his assistant Kringe, in "a lavish hidden bunker complex" in "the hills surrounding the [small] town." Mister Hotline and Kring work for an organization known as "the *Brotherhood of Hades*." It's almost as if Kirby's *trying* to throw every super-hero cliché at readers.

We discover that these villains work for a boss called the Monitor, who appears like a demon in a room that, concurrent with the Monitor's arrival, bursts into flames. The organization's goal, as Mister Hotline puts it, is "*universal mind control!*" The Monitor explains that he wants to probe Mister Machine in order to discover the "secret" that will give him "the power to control *all* living things!" It's not clear *how* he'll learn this from Mister Machine, except the vague idea that Mister Machine is an android, so maybe he has the "secret" to life itself – which, once figured out, would magically let the Monitor control the minds of everyone on Earth. It's nonsensical, but it strongly echoes Darkseid's search for the Anti-Life Equation, in Kirby's own *New Gods* (which had also been prematurely cancelled, earlier in the 1970s).

Mister Machine, Jerry, and Olivia repose at the home of Judge Franklin Fields. Olivia's last name is Fields, but it's immediately not clear if she's visiting the judge, or if she's his wife or daughter. This is only one of the story's many ambiguities – which unlike the ambiguities of Kubrick's *2001* don't exist for any discernable purpose. Only on the final page do we learn that the judge is Jerry's father, making him Olivia's sister. It's never made clear what happened to Jerry's mother, nor does this affect the plot in any obvious way. We may guess that Jerry's attachment to super-heroes and to Mister Machine is related to his mother's death, but this is mere conjecture – and Kirby doesn't explore the potential implications.

Despite Mister Machine refusing to give Olivia any answers at the end of the previous issue, he's happy to tell the judge that he considers Abel Stack his father. The judge informs Mister Machine of Stack's death, which upsets the super-hero.

Then goons from the Brotherhood of Hades arrive, and soon Mister Machine is brought before Mister Hotline. He resists, but the threat to Jerry, Olivia, and the judge is enough to make him submit. The goons put Mister Machine into a tank, and he's imprisoned again — much as he was by the military, two issues previously. There, he swore he'd never let himself be imprisoned again, but he makes no reference to that event.

Technicians cut Mister Machine into pieces, separating his head and limbs from his torso. Is this a metaphor for how Kirby's science-fiction comic was also disassembled? Can we also see it as a metaphor for how Kirby's *2001* was divided against itself, as a science-fiction comic questioning human identity and spanning human history, yet produced by the last person who ought to be producing such a comic?

Mister Hotline takes Mister Machine's head to the room in which the Monitor materializes — which the Satanic villain promptly does, announcing, "Prepare to yield that which is *free will*!" The Monitor then probes Mister Machine's decapitated head — producing a great visual that echoes cartoonish images of electrocution, in which a skeleton is visible.

Tellingly, when the Satanic-looking Monitor materializes before Mister Machine's head, Mister Machine thinks, "By all the old *cliches! He wants my soul!*" It seems to be a comment about the villain's appearance and goal, but it could equally be a commentary on Kirby's more general reversion to super-hero clichés, including the Monitor but extending far beyond that villain.

Under attack by Mister Machine, the new super-hero sends a signal out to his detached limbs. Cameras sprout from each of them, and they hilariously duke it out with the technicians before reattaching to Mister Machine's torso. Before the cult's soldiers can fire on the door to the lab, Mister Machine's decapitated body bursts out, another camera having sprouted from where his head should be, and crashes through to the android's head. It's a wonderful sequence — and pure Kirby. When Kirby's plots go astray, as this story has, they *really* go astray. But when the uncontrolled artist excels in a sequence such as this, he *really* excels.

After reattaching his head to his body, Mister Machine blasts the Monitor — who disappears, having been only a hologram. The blast blows a hole in the wall, through which Mister Machine discovers "a *super-computer!* With the potential to *rule* the world!"

It's another nice turn in an already failed story. A villainous computer makes a perfect adversary for Mister Machine. It also raises the possibility that the Monitor only wanted to discover the secret of Mister Machine's sentience. But Kirby doesn't explore the possibility. Nor does he even explain how this *"super-computer"* would gain the ability to control every mind on Earth by examining Mister Machine. Revealing that the Monitor is itself a computer *feels* right poetically, but it doesn't make the illogical story make any more sense.

Using the Monitor's screens, Mister Machine is able to see the Fields family, held hostage by a single goon with explosive strapped to his chest, like some super-villain version of a suicide bomber. Mister Machine reprograms the Monitor, and we soon see the result: the goon is electrocuted into unconsciousness, and the bomb on his chest disintegrates into "dry *powder!*" Typically, it's not clear *how* the bomb could disintegrate in this way. Olivia calls the sheriff, while the judge gets rope to bind the goon before he awakes. Jerry says he's "going to write a letter to Marvel Comics and tell them all about it."

That's slightly clever, and it seems to further indicate that super-heroes don't exist in this universe – despite that Marvel would later retroactively place this story within the Marvel Universe. But it's worth remembering that, while this universe's Marvel Comics might not know of any real-life super-heroes, it still inhabits a universe filled with super-villain organizations with underground lairs and holograms and copious uniformed goons – a universe in which the military is creating thinking androids and scientists have anti-gravity technology. This Marvel Comics might be in a world without super-heroes, but Mister Machine's emergence doesn't *cause* the Monitor or the Brotherhood of Hades to come into existence. This universe has been deformed into a silly super-hero one long before Mister Machine's arrival.

Sadly, we don't ever get to see the sheriff again. Last we saw him, he'd been challenged to find the wreckage of those flying eggs, and he acted as if the judge was a local big-shot. It would therefore be nice to follow up on this character – but Kirby doesn't.

We also don't ever see Mister Machine return to Jerry and Olivia. Nor will they appear in Kirby's *Machine Man*. Mister Machine just leaves them.

We also haven't seen Dr. Broadhurst or Col. Kragg again, nor follow up on the *"homing device"* Broadhurst had affixed to Mister Machine – the story simply drops all of this, although they *would* reappear in Kirby's *Machine Man*.

Instead, we only see Mister Machine flying out of the Brotherhood of Hades's bunker – which is connected to an above-ground portion, prompting us to wonder why the sheriff or others haven't seen it. As Mister Machine escapes, it explodes – due to Mister Machine's reprogramming of the Monitor, which he only two pages said could "be *rehabilitated* to perform some good deeds!" Instead, he's only programmed the computer to self-destruct.

That's right: having discovered an advanced computer that was doing things he didn't like, Mister Machine simply blew it up. Ironically, this duplicates what Kragg wants to do to Mister Machine – who's now killed the Monitor, despite admitting it could be reprogrammed for good. But if the story's aware of this irony, it doesn't show it. We're supposed to be content with the Monitor's destruction, because it's the bad guy, and super-heroes like Mister Machine can't do wrong.

We also don't see the various minions of the Brotherhood of Hades again, nor Mister Hotline and Kringe – all of whom were presumably killed by Mister Machine, when he caused the Monitor to explode.

Instead, the story teases future adventures. Mister Machine guesses that "whoever built the *Mind Monitor* as the center of a Devil-worshipping cult is an evil *genius* with dreams too big to have been Mister Hotline!" But Kirby wouldn't be following up on this either, in his *Machine Man*.

The next issue blurb is an advertisement for this new title – although it still refers to the hero as Mister Machine. When the new series debuted seven months later (#1, Apr 1978), it and Mister Machine would be renamed.

And that's it for Jack Kirby's *2001, A Space Odyssey* – the weirdest sci-fi comic ever made. If there were ever an indication that Jack Kirby should never have continued the movie by Stanley Kubrick, it's that this continuation descended into a super-hero title after all. Kirby might not have wanted to be limited to the role of super-hero comics creator. But despite some great heights along the way, he couldn't escape the clichés he mocked. And in the end, he embraced them after all.

Kirby's *2001* didn't lead to an odd version of the *2001* universe, with the Monolith guiding human society far more than in the movie, and with these literal star babies cruising about the galaxies. Kirby didn't end up revealing the alien society that created the Monoliths, nor reveal what the agenda was in creating these star babies. The David Bowman star child never returned, nor did the various star children team up. All of this might have been informed by super-hero tropes, but it would have been fascinating. Kirby's *2001* didn't lead to these things. In fact, it flails about in interesting and sometimes misguided ways. But it ultimately led Kirby back to his real métier: the super-hero comic, in all its clichéd, illogical, and bombastic glory.

Perhaps the saddest missed opportunity in this final story is that, while it smartly gives Mister Machine a super-computer for an opponent, it doesn't realize that this tale of a machine struggling with its human creators reflects the original movie's HAL 9000.

Earlier, we discussed how HAL offers a kind the bridge between the movie's outer-space sequences and its more existential or even metaphysical concerns. The film's beginning and ending chapters seem to be about the Monolith and the destiny of humanity – and what humanity is capable of finding or even becoming, among the stars. But this central portion, known for its realistic depiction of space travel, is also famous for HAL, which represents humanity playing the role of the Monolith and creating or guiding artificial life. This parallel breaks down in the film, however, because HAL isn't treated by the Monolith as a life form worthy of intervention; he's ultimately just a tool, and it's impossible to reconcile this with the existential sequences focusing on the glories of *human* evolution.

In continuing this story, Kirby focused on those existential concerns, and his initial formula for the ongoing *2001* omitted the long middle part of the film entirely, as if this were mere tedium between the trippy beginning and ending of the movie. Even when Kirby turned to 2040, he focused on super-heroes and a wacky story of the (as far as we know) first human to visit another galaxy, not on the slow progress of the space program. Clarke, on the other hand, extrapolated upon the outer-space sequences, depicting the future progress of humanity in outer space, and ended up relegating the transformation of David Bowman to the recording of his personality onto the Monolith, which Clarke made simply a complex computer.

In this final story, Kirby also told an existential tale. Fundamentally, this is the story of an android coming to terms with its humanity, rejecting the villainous and fearful parts of that humanity while championing the good it sees. We might be tempted to see this as a sort of redemption of HAL 9000, who turned against the Discovery One's crew. Except that Kirby doesn't seem to have made the connection, and Mister Machine's story is far more concerned with super-hero tropes than with any conscious mirroring of HAL. Kirby, like Clarke, wasn't able to escape his own predelictions as a writer.

Still, it's at least *evocative* that Kirby's story ended up concerning itself with artificial intelligence. It came around to this crucial, unresolved element of the original film. But so great was Kirby's training, or his own predelicions, that even this could only gesture vaguely in this direction, not tie things together.

Kirby's *2001* is a failure. It is occasionally a wonderful comic, on its own terms – here, one cannot help but think of issues #5-6. But it isn't a very good *2001* comic at all. Although, by its conclusion, it gestures towards what one might have been.

Consider how easy it would have been, to have shown, at a key point in the narrative, that the X-models were built with a red eye inside them, similar to HAL's famous console. The cameras Mister Machine's limbs sprout could even have been built in a similar design. The idea could have been that we're seeing a predecessor to HAL.

And how about tying the creator of the Monitor into the equation? Its name even recalls the Monolith, as well as the title of Clarke's short story, "The Sentinel," that inspired *2001*.

Or Kirby could have set the story in 2001 after all, with at most minor changes – such as perhaps replacing Dr. Broadhurst or Dr. Stack with Dr. Chandra, mentioned in the novel version of *2001* as HAL's programmer (and featured in Clarke's *2010: Odyssey Two*). HAL 9000 could itself have put in an appearance, in either a prequel or a sequel to the original movie.

And if artificial intelligence offers a bridge between the two largely unconnected aspects of the original movie, it also offers a metaphor for fictional creation. As creators, neither Kirby nor Clarke could ultimately steer their continuations coherently. Instead, both continuations reflected the strengths and weaknesses of their creators. Like HAL and Mister Machine, both men's continuations stubbornly refused to follow the perimeters of their original design.

Speculations about what Kirby *might* have done, if he had only seen the possibilities, aren't really creative second-guessing. In fact, they illustrate the greatest strength of Kirby's continuation. Sure, it's a failure – both as a continuation of *2001* and largely even on their own terms. But it at least demonstrates the *potential* for a franchise set in the same universe as *2001*. And if there's one thing Kirby's *2001* demonstrates, beyond Kirby's own tendencies and limits as an artist, it's the profound potential of the series.

As flabbergasting as it might sound, the revered film really *could* have been adapted into a franchise. The fact that Kirby's comic failed to do so is perhaps less shocking than that it was good and interesting enough to suggest how such a *2001* franchise might, in defiance of the odds, actually have been developed.

About the Author

After graduating *magna cum laude* from Lawrence University (Appleton, Wisconsin), Dr. Julian Darius obtained his M.A. in English, authoring a thesis on John Milton and utopianism. In 2002, he moved to Waikiki, teaching college while obtaining an M.A. in French (high honors) and a Ph.D. in English.

His controversial dissertation became the novel *Nira/Sussa*. Darius has authored other works of fiction, including *Watching People Burn*, a screenplay based on the true story of the deadliest school massacre in U.S history – which occurred in rural Michigan in 1927.

In 1996, while still an undergraduate, Darius founded what would become Sequart Research & Literacy Organization (Sequart.org), an organization devoted to promoting comic books as a legitimate art form. He writes for Sequart's website, has authored books on *Batman Begins* and classic DC Comics stories, and has produced documentary films for the organization.

He currently lives in Illinois.

Also from Sequart

CLASSICS ON INFINITE EARTHS: THE JUSTICE LEAGUE AND DC CROSSOVER CANON

THE DEVIL IS IN THE DETAILS: EXAMINING MATT MURDOCK AND DAREDEVIL

TEENAGERS FROM THE FUTURE: ESSAYS ON THE LEGION OF SUPER-HEROES

GOTHAM CITY 14 MILES: 14 ESSAYS ON WHY THE 1960S BATMAN TV SERIES MATTERS

IMPROVING THE FOUNDATIONS: *BATMAN BEGINS* FROM COMICS TO SCREEN

MUTANT CINEMA: THE X-MEN TRILOGY FROM COMICS TO SCREEN

GRANT MORRISON: THE EARLY YEARS

OUR SENTENCE IS UP: SEEING GRANT MORRISON'S *THE INVISIBLES*

CURING THE POSTMODERN BLUES: READING GRANT MORRISON AND CHRIS WESTON'S *THE FILTH* IN THE 21ST CENTURY

AND THE UNIVERSE SO BIG: UNDERSTANDING *BATMAN: THE KILLING JOKE*

KEEPING THE WORLD STRANGE: A *PLANETARY* GUIDE

MINUTES TO MIDNIGHT: TWELVE ESSAYS ON *WATCHMEN*

For more information and for exclusive content, visit Sequart.org.

Printed in Great Britain
by Amazon